Voices Worth the Listening

Voices Worth the Listening
Three Women of Appalachia

Thomas Burton

The University of Tennessee Press
Knoxville

Library of Congress Cataloging-in-Publication Data
Names: Burton, Thomas G., author.
Title: Voices worth the listening : three women of Appalachia / Thomas
  Burton.
Description: First edition. | Knoxville : The University of Tennessee
  Press, 2020. | Includes bibliographical references and index. | Summary:
  "Based on recorded interviews with three different women in different
  parts of Appalachia, Thomas Burton's carefully crafted oral history
  lends a timely ear to the lives of three contemporary Appalachian women
  recounted in their own words. Essentialist stereotypes and misplaced
  debates about Appalachian character are never far from any study of this
  region's people, but as readers will find here, individuals who dwell in the
  region have stories of their own to tell, each one differing from the other,
  insisting on a fresh hearing" —Provided by publisher.
Identifiers: LCCN 2019057957 (print) | LCCN 2019057958 (ebook) |
  ISBN 9781621905578 (paperback) | ISBN 9781621905851 (pdf)
Subjects: LCSH: Women—Appalachian Region—Biography. | Appalachians
  (People) —Biography. | Appalachian Region—Social life and customs. |
  Oral history.
Classification: LCC F106 .B944 2020 (print) | LCC F106 (ebook) |
  DDC 305.40974—dc23
LC record available at https://lccn.loc.gov/2019057957
LC ebook record available at https://lccn.loc.gov/2019057958

Contents

Foreword

"Lord, I'd like to be world-class at something / I'm not sure it would matter so much in what."[1] So begins a wistful poem by Thomas Burton, the collector/editor of this remarkable trio of portraits.

I have been a fan of Thomas Burton's published work for a very long time now, and I would like to propose to him a paradox: Tom, you are indeed world class: you have a world-class ear for the distinctive voices of the seemingly undistinguished. Further, you have a genius for presenting these voices on the page in such a way that the rest of us can hear the distinction—the music—in your interviewees' ruminations on their lives. The lives of the women represented here have not been easy: full of false starts, errors, ugliness, tragedy both inevitable and accidental. Their moments of self-awareness seem at best intermittent. Their circumstances are the stuff of a sociologist's dream, hedged with social, financial, educational, and psychological limits, and burdened with a kind of regional fatalism that is currently the source of vigorous academic and popular debate among pundits of Appalachian culture. It is your gift that, invisible yourself, you present these life stories in such a way that the women emerge through their own words fully dimensional, moving, and oddly triumphant. So in the remainder of this short essay, I'd like to pull you from behind the curtain, and talk to your readers about your accomplishment. Perhaps shifting from the second- to third-person pronouns (with a little of my own first-person thrown in) will embarrass you less—anyway, here goes.

Thomas Burton is perhaps best known for his contributions to the study of Appalachian folk culture, such as *Serpent-Handling Believers* (Univ. of Tennessee Press, 1993), *The Serpent and the Spirit: Glenn Summerford's Story* (Univ. of Tennessee Press, 2004), and *Beech Mountain Man: The Memoirs of Ronda Lee Hicks* (Univ. of Tennessee Press, 2009). In addition, he is an accomplished poet and author of the narrative *Michael and the War in Heaven* (Overmountain Press, 2016), a most extraordinary work of fantasy fiction. Readers of the two works on serpent handlers and the memoir of notable badass Ronda Lee Hicks will have discerned Burton's fascination with mavericks and outliers, whom he represents both unsparingly and with a certain astonished empathy. But he also transcribed and edited the delightful *Rosie Hicks and Her Recipe Book* (LandaBooks, 2013), a combined memoir and recipe collection of a woman best known to outsiders as the wife of Ray Hicks, the famed storyteller and National Heritage

Award Fellow. Burton describes her affectionately as "a genteel woman whose gentle speech is the product of the mountain environment of which she is a part."[2] The life accounts comprising this current collection engage both the tenderness of Burton's treatment of Rosie Hicks and the revelations of moral ambiguity (to say the least) in his rigorous works concerning Glenn Summerford and Ronda Lee Hicks. These representations come to the reader with a minimum of editorial comment and accompanying documentation, allowing the voices of his subjects to shine.

General readers familiar with other forms of oral history, such as those by Studs Terkel, will not find this self-effacing approach striking. On the other hand, scholars trained in the ethnographic disciplines—such as anthropology, sociology, and especially folk studies in recent decades—may find it arresting, even downright subversive. Folklore scholar Richard M. Dorson scented winds of disciplinary change in 1973, when he suspiciously dubbed junior colleagues who insisted on full, "thick" contextual documentation of oral narrative the Young Turks. "Texts and annotations will be subordinated to close analyses of group dynamics and psychocultural relationships," he averred,[3] and the threat of revolution he detected in this subordination was rapidly picked up by other scholars whose battle-cry response to the new approach was "The Text Is the Thing!"[4] This dispute is largely forgotten; ethnographic documentation now routinely includes contextual and textural information as detailed as the make of the tape recorder used, the weather on the day in question, and the subjective response of the interviewer to the encounter. Burton's lean presentation of text brings the reader back to the speakers.

This is not to say that their voices are unmediated. I have been transcribing audio recordings since my late teens and have taught conventions of professional transcription to graduate students in my discipline for nearly thirty years— and I am persuaded that there is an art to the process that goes well beyond a good ear and accurate spelling skills. A gifted editor/transcriber makes the speaker's voice leap from the page through innumerable small choices: punctuation, paragraphing, treatment of nonstandard word pronunciation, and a host of other elements that characterize the processes of a sensitive individual who is not just hearing the speaker, but who is actively listening.

Burton himself was the interviewer as well as the transcriber in encounters presented in this collection—not always the case in his previous published works. We do not know the questions that elicited such frank and revealing responses, but we know most certainly that he shaped an atmosphere of trust in which three women not accustomed to a Socratic "examined life" reach an extraordinary degree of circumstantial detail and critical self-revelation.

In reading Burton's rendering of these three accounts, I was reminded of two other exceptionally adroit listeners, both outside my disciplinary boundaries. I came to know the works of Henry Mayhew, the nineteenth-century chronicler of London street life, just as my academic training began, and the four volumes of his masterwork *London Labour and the London Poor* (Griffin, Bohn, and Co., 1861) have remained within reach at my bedside ever since. Along with his own trenchant observations, he included lengthy testimony concerning life and work from the lips of his interviewees—surely reconstructed from notes and memory, but resounding with the authentic note of distinctive human individuals.

> "Ay indeed," said another book-stall keeper [of dubious publications], "anything scarce or curious, when it's an old book, is kept out of the streets; if it's not particular decent, sir," (with a grin), "why it's reckoned all the more curious,—that's the word, sir, I know,—'curious.' I can tell how many beans make five as well as you or anybody."[5]

The reader can almost smell the fellow, and count the teeth in his leer, so clearly is his voice represented by Mayhew's skill. Having read and reread the three narratives in this collection, I likewise have the strong impression I could pick each one out of a crowd, based on accounts that seem less like the product of a focused inquiry than a self-prompted introspective interior monologue.

Another writer who, on the evidence, must have mastered the art of deep listening was William Shakespeare. Along with the generic bag of tricks of the Elizabethan playwright he shared with Christopher Marlowe and Ben Jonson, Shakespeare had a unique gift for portraying an occasional ruminative break in tone and action, in which the speaker seems to be neither in dialogue with other characters on stage nor in soliloquy with the audience.

So, reflecting in parallel her own confusion, Desdemona recalls:

> My mother had a maid call'd Barbary;
> She was in love, and he she lov'd prov'd mad,
> And did forsake her. She had a song of "Willow,"
> An old thing 'twas, but it express'd her fortune,
> And she died singing it.
>
> (*Othello* 4.3)

Mistress Quickly recounts in garrulous but heartbreaking detail the death of Falstaff more effectively than any staged deathbed scene could convey:

> 'A made a finer end, and went away and it had been any christom child. 'A parted ev'n just between twelve and one, ev'n at the turning o' th' tide . . .
>
> (*Henry V* 2.3)

And the terrified soldier Williams broods on the horror of what he takes to be his own impending death by resorting to philosophy of the trenches:

> . . . if the cause be not good, the King himself hath a heavy reckoning to make, when all those legs and arms and heads, chopp'd off in a battle, shall join together at the latter day and cry all, "We died at such a place"—some swearing, some crying for a surgeon, some upon their wives left poor behind them, some upon the debts they owe, some upon their children rawly left. I am afeard there are few die well that die in a battle . . .
>
> (*Henry V* 4.1)

It is the largesse of Shakespeare as supreme listener/creator that he created these moments for characters who are gentle, but not necessarily genteel—even the well-born Desdemona is recounting in her reverie the betrayal and downfall of a young serving maid, as expressed through a banal little folk song that "express'd her fortune."

Thomas Burton offers a like gift in the accounts in this publication—a gift both to his readers and to the women whose lives he chronicles in their own words. They are women who, one feels, might be seen any day of the week at the grocery or bus stop or in the halls of one's place of work. But in Burton's hands, their response to repeated betrayals, lengthy confusions, brief triumphs, and failed or successful strategies of endurance, all finally appear moving, monumental and memorable.

And I suggest that Tom Burton's achievement in this work, and the many that precede it, is truly *world class.*

—Erika Brady, Professor of Folk Studies,
Western Kentucky University

Notes

1. Thomas Burton, "On Being World Class," *Doubting Thomas's Book of Common Prayers* (Georgetown, KY: Finishing Line Press, 2016), 22.

2. Thomas Burton in Donnie Henderson Shedlarz, *Rosie Hicks and Her Recipe Book,* ed. Thomas Burton (Winston-Salem, NC: LandaBooks, 2013), xii.

3 Richard M. Dorson, *Folklore and Folklife* (Chicago: University of Chicago Press, 1973), 47.

4. D. K. Wilgus, "The Text Is the Thing," *Journal of American Folklore* 86, no. 341 (1973): 241–52. For a concise discussion of the dispute, see Lisa Gabbert, "The Text/Context Controversy and the Emergence of Behavioral Approaches in Folklore," *Folklore Forum* 30, no. 1/2 (1999): 119–28, and, most recently, Simon Bronner "Toward a Definition of Folklore in Practice," *Cultural Analysis* 15, no. 1 (2016): 6–27.

5. Henry Mayhew, *London Labour and the London Poor*, vol. 1 (London: Griffin, Bohn, and Co., 1861), 293.

Preface

The three portraits presented in the following pages
are derived from multiple, personally taped interviews with the subjects. The names of the three
individuals interviewed, place-names, and many
other specifically identifying details are omitted
or obscured to prevent any negative repercussions
for the individuals from the telling of their stories.
The portraits are not versions of detailed linguis-
tic transcriptions denoting accurately the varied
aspects of each speaker's use of language, which
would produce assuredly somewhat unreadable
texts for the general reader. Neither are the portraits abstracts of straightforward transcriptions,
minimally edited as I was once naively asked of
a friend regarding a manuscript: "You know, just
correct the grammar or any misspelled words and
make it read smoothly." The objective in these portraits is entirely different.

Extended, informal conversation is not characterized by an unhesitating, coherent, unified, progressive, and non-repetitious expression of thought. And comprehension of recorded conversation is not complemented, as in face-to-face conversation, by gestures, facial expressions, personal knowledge of the speaker, and a number of other communicative means. Speakers use, normally without clarification, different varieties of language in different cultural contexts; that is, they have different registers. These registers can be more glaring in print than in personal audience, and readers can easily jump to wrong conclusions regarding intelligence—even morality—without proper perspective of the speaker's registers. I have kept in mind these and other factors of personal conversation in presenting the three portraits—although I leave the matter of register primarily to the reader's empathetic judgment. I have attempted not just to clean up transcriptions of the interviews, but to craft amalgamations of them into meaningful, intelligible monologues while retaining as much as possible through all alterations the integrity of each person's speech and meaning. It is, of course, impossible for me to recreate in print the experience of personally listening to these women; but to the degree that I can, I offer the reader voices of three women, revealing stories of themselves—and indirectly of other women similar to them—voices worth the listening.

Acknowledgments

I am foremost deeply indebted to the three women who have trusted and permitted me to record and publish the forthright telling of their private stories. There are also friends and colleagues who have been significant in the production of this work, namely: Roberta Herrin, John Taylor, John Smith, Rolly Harwell, William Haston (professional educators who contributed valuable consultation); Joey Whitlock (a detective who clarified policing details); Lauren Brown, Judy Parker, and David Hatcher (friends who proofed the manuscript); and the ETSU Information Technology Services (which resolved computer issues). Particularly important to my work has been the use of a locked carrel in Sherrod Library, provided by Patricia Van Zandt, former dean of East Tennessee State University Libraries. To these and others unnamed, I heartily express my appreciation.

Voices Worth the Listening

Introduction

Years back a colleague, new to me and to the area, asked as the two of us were walking down a flight of steps in one of the university buildings, "You've been out among these people in Appalachia—what makes them 'tick'?" I was taken aback and quipped: "Well, there are wood ticks and there are clocks that tick." His reaction was: "You're really a smart-aleck." Maybe I was, but I was smart enough to know that the people of Appalachia are so diverse and complicated that the question "What makes Appalachians 'tick'?" is wrongheaded. It erroneously implies that the essence of Appalachia and its people as a *whole* can be absolutely perceived and succinctly delineated. Shibboleths of course are suggested, for example "coal," as one professor suggested to me years ago. "Poverty" is perhaps the one most commonly heard currently, along with, among others, "sense of place," "welfare dependency," "kinship," "violence," "siege mentality," "self-reliance," "Cracker culture," and various forms of "bigotry."

Appalachia is better viewed as part of the country shaped not only by its geologic evolution, but also by the total geographic evolution of its diverse internal areas, particularly the evolution of the cultures of the human inhabitants in these areas, i.e., of their beliefs, values, traditions, work, etc. When I first began to do research in the mountains of western North Carolina, I tended to think of that area as representing "Appalachia." But I soon learned that although the lives of mountain folk in that area were similar to the lives of mountain folk in nearby Southwest Virginia and Kentucky, they were also significantly different from them. And, of course, that dichotomy was true relative to the other mountainous areas of Appalachia. Also in my representative model, I failed to take into account the other areas of Appalachia: piedmont, valley, rural, urban, etc. To me the culture of Appalachia is so diverse and complex that the area as a whole or in part lends itself to an *analysis of its culture* rather than to a *delineation of its essence.*

Instead of the quip to my colleague, I might well have alluded to Hamlet's response to two of his associates, "Why, look you now, how unworthy a thing you make of me! . . . you would pluck out the heart of my mystery." And, to follow Hamlet's imagery, "there is much music, excellent voice in" Appalachia. But all too often, people don't listen to those voices, as I have found repeatedly in my research.

A case in point relates to a group identified as Pentecostal Holiness Sign Followers. Members of this contemporary religious group, apparently originating in Southern Appalachia but not exclusively unique to it, are viewed sometimes as crazy snake handlers or even snake worshipers. I have found, however, that regardless of varied individual responses to them, many instances of their religious rituals are performed without bodily harm and their beliefs evidently prove efficacious physically, spiritually, and socially. For example, church members have participated without apparent harm in rituals, such as contacting sources of heat exceeding 675 degrees Fahrenheit, handling venomous serpents, and consuming possibly lethal doses of poison. Additionally their faith has resulted in worshipers' being apparently restored to health from minor and mortal diseases and being redeemed from lives of desperation. And "how unworthy a thing" is made of other Appalachians by those who do not listen carefully to the voices of the "hillbillies," "rednecks," "trailer white trash," "niggers," "illegal aliens," "Confederate-heritage preservationists," "Bible-Belt bigots," "trolls," "underserved," and various other demeaningly or questionably labeled members of Appalachia.

I have had the opportunity to research, personally interview, and present in different media various voices of Appalachians, e.g., tradition bearers of varied knowledge and skills, true believers, railroaders, convicts, and bikers. These voices have been primarily from the area north from Kentucky and southwest Virginia, southward through northern Georgia and Alabama, east from the Blue Ridge Mountains of North Carolina westward through Tennessee. Some of these individuals were from the mountains, others from coalfields, cities, towns, and adjoining rural communities. Some came from impoverished situations, others from subsistent and much better circumstances. Diverse voices—all a part of Appalachia.

In the text that follows, I present portraits of three women of Appalachia. Their voices, of course, do not tell what makes Appalachians "tick"; they do not pluck out the elusive mystery of themselves or of others similar to them. They are assuredly not unique to Appalachia, but listening to them does provide revelations that contribute to the comprehension of three interesting humans who are somewhat representative of a certain limitedly assessed stratum of Appalachians composed of women who have lived much or all of their lives out of the mainstream.

Incidentally, I knew initially very little of this stratum and was perplexed by it; fortuitously, I had the opportunity to learn more and, consequently, was able to expand my understanding of Appalachia and Appalachians. My wish is that listening to these women will have much the same effect upon the readers, who in many cases, I suspect, have little or no previous knowledge of similar lives.

The Portraits

When you read the dramatic stories of these women, I suggest that you listen carefully to their voices, which evoke both specific and general insights about themselves as well as about certain aspects of the culture of which they are a part. Or, if you will, follow each of the women as though you were having the opportunity and privilege (without a critic at your side) to watch a player present her own private role "as 'twere the mirror up to nature."

Some Would Call Her a Good Old Girl

Portrait: a white woman, born in 1971 in self-
sufficient circumstances, who was reared as a child
in a county of ca. 74,000 population. As an adult,
she has lived in the same general area in neighboring small cities and towns. Her formal education
includes the completion of elementary school, the
beginning of high school (a county school, ca. 900
enrollment), and the attainment of a high school
equivalency certificate. She is the mother of three
sons.

Notable Personae: mother, aunt, great uncle, husbands,
mother-in-law, sister-in-law, children, boyfriends,
and girlfriends.

Themes (among others): family background, religious
influence, effects of personal appearance, control
by others, self-blame, behavior justification, self-
esteem, financial aid, self-knowledge, peer influence, work ethic, maternal-parent fidelity, marital
expectation and relationship, maternal instinct,

> caregiving, manipulation by and of males, gender
> roles, physical/mental abuse, naïveté, alcoholism,
> partying, sexual conduct, homelessness, neuroses,
> regret, and survival.

I don't have a roof over my head. I was kicked out by my
ex-sister-in-law and went to stay with an old girlfriend,
but then I had to leave there too because of some compli-
cations. I'm going over to another friend's house where he
said I could sleep on the couch. It's better than being back
on the streets like I once was. All of this is really my fault
for a lot of bad decisions over many years. But things didn't
start this way for me.

I was brought up by my mother with my grandparents.
I didn't have a father growing up—I never knew my father.
My grandparents, they passed away when I was seven years
old, but I have good memories of them. My grandfather
wanted me to be a boy, so he tried to raise me as a tomboy,
planting gardens and whittling. He had a tobacco and cattle
farm. My grandmother had me peeling apples for canning
when I was three years old (I remember cutting my finger
wide open). And I used to go get eggs with her. And my
grandfather would take me fishing. We had a pond way
back in the field, the cattle field. My family were church
people, First Baptists. Every Sunday and Wednesday and
revival we were at church. I was in the church choir, played
bells; and anything going on at church, my mom and I were
involved.

Now, my mother's folks lived about fifteen miles away—I

had a lot of family there—we had some good times. I try to remember my good times over my bad ones. Every Sunday my great uncle—he won a Subaru with bucket seats in the back which he won from Mello Yello—and every Sunday, I'd hop in the back of that Subaru. My mom and him would get in the front, and we'd go and visit my mother's family. There was probably about fifteen or twenty of us. We'd all get together, and they'd cook a big ol' Sunday dinner. We'd have badminton in the backyard or play cards. My other uncle would play the banjo, and we'd clog. Or we would go to the recreation park and go swimming. That's the good part.

As I said, I didn't have a father. My mother messed around with a married man and ended up with me. Come to find out later on, when I was like twelve, thirteen years old, that he, my half sister, and half brother actually lived right down the road from us. Without knowing it, I rode a bus with them. A long time after that, I contacted him twice. The first time was when I had my first son, and he denied that I was his daughter. I let it go at that. Then when his father died, I contacted him again. That time he cussed me out and told me never to come call on him again. He said I was not his daughter—and he was just "effin" us and "eff" that. Yeah, it was bad. I also remember vaguely that I did meet his mother when I was little. My mom used to take me over to his mother's house, I guess just to show her who I was. I don't even know if she's alive anymore or my father.

It bothered me not having a father, yeah, especially in school. You have to fill out that paperwork, where they say "mother's name, father's name." And it was embarrassing when your friends have fathers and you don't. It's hard when someone says, "What's your dad do?" And you're like, "I don't know." My mom didn't tell me about my father until later on in life. She just always told me that *she* was my father and mother; and that's what I told everyone. School was traumatic for me. I got bullied a lot. I was overweight and the shortest one. I wore glasses, and they called me Four Eyes and Mole Eye because then I had a mole growing on my eyelid. Everyone made fun of my name by making vulgar puns on it. It was horrible. I was also shy, a loner, and had few friends.

There were also problems at home—I grew up with alcoholics. My Aunt Lou, my mom's sister, was an alcoholic; and she would also take pills. She was jealous of me, partly because my mom's uncle sort of spoiled me a little bit. I guess he became my father figure when my grandparents passed away. He too was a really bad alcoholic. He had worked at one time for NASA at the Kennedy Space Center on the very first space shuttle that went into space. He lived in Florida, but he would come and live with us during the summers. He would buy me things and do other little things for me. My aunt said I had him wrapped around my little finger.

When I was just five years old, my aunt chased me around the house with a kitchen butcher knife. She was really drinking and high on pills. She said she was gonna kill me. My mom locked me in my grandparents' bedroom, and my aunt took that knife and stabbed holes in the door.

When my mother finally let me out of the room, the next thing I know, my mom was struggling with her to take away the knife. My mom was able to get the knife, but my aunt kept at her and in the process was stabbed in the stomach. My aunt didn't die, but the cops came and took my mom to jail. If it hadn't been for me speaking out and saying she saved my life, my mom probably would have gone to jail for a very long time.

Besides being an alcoholic, my uncle had a lot of strokes, and I would have to go around cleaning up his drool. My grandparents became bedridden, and both had catheters. My mother got hospital beds, twin beds, for them and put the beds in their room. Even at five, I would feed them, bathe them, clothe them, and help my mother take care of them until we couldn't anymore. That's pretty much what I've done all my life, take care of people. I don't know if that's what God's meant for me, but sometimes I feel like that might be a part of what He's wanting me to do now.

When I was about thirteen, fourteen, I started rebelling against my mother. She wouldn't let me go and hang out with my friends and let me be a teenager. She kept me close in the house; so when I was able to get out, I went a little bit crazy and wild on her. I shouldn't have rebelled like that, and I wish I could go back and change things now. I got into alcohol and marijuana. I was hanging around with the wrong crowd. The first guy I dated, I actually met in the church that my grandmother went to. I come to find out he was a troublemaker, into mischief; and his parents wanted me in his life to try to straighten him out. But he corrupted me. I shouldn't say that. The drinking and the marijuana was there and he offered it and I didn't say no. He was a churchgoer and his parents were churchgoers and he'd been in and out of drug rehabilitation. And my mom really didn't want me hanging out with him. She knew all this, I didn't. But his parents thought it would be good for us to hang out, that maybe I could straighten him out. And now that's the way it happened. He introduced me to a lot of drugs, a lot of bad drugs, pills, cocaine, acid. Yeah . . . did a lot of tripping. And it was bad. And one time sex was involved—I did have sex with him. We weren't even dating at the time, since I had started dating another boy, Jake, that he in fact introduced me to—the one I was to marry. So I had cheated on Jake and regretted it and still regret it. On the night it happened, Jake left me and a girlfriend of mine with this boy in a warehouse. Jake was a drummer in a band and took off to a practice. We all ended up getting drunk and just doing stupid stuff that night—my girlfriend was into the same thing as me. We went back to this guy's place and doing something that was not appropriate. I really got into trouble with my mother over it because I didn't come home till like two or three in the morning, and she was worried to death about me. I came in with hickeys all over my neck, and she threatened to send me to an all-girls' school.

That incident hurt the relationship with Jake, but we ended making up. He was really pissed. I'd never done anything like that before; and after we made up, I have never, willing, had multiple sex partners. I never have slept with a lot of men. I slept with that one guy (my very first) on one night along with this other girl that I grew up with. And I slept with Jake. He also would get me to have sex with him along with that girl several evenings when we'd be swimming naked in a neighbor's swimming pool. She always wanted him. Last year I just got being friends with her again— I'm forty-five, and we've known each other for thirty-three years. But she used me once more; and now, I's like, I'm done with her. She's still in the drug scene, and I just can't be around it. She says she isn't, that she's clean, but not from my end. I don't see it. I just can't be around that. You got to grow up sometime.

About a few months down the road after that incident with my girlfriend, I found out that I was pregnant by Jake. I had no idea until I started to show. My mom was furious. It flew all over her. She didn't even know I was sexually active. She actually waited too late to tell me about the birds and the bees. My mom said I had a lot going in my life and that I didn't need a baby. She said I was too young, and I was. But I would not abide by my mom's wishes. She wanted me to have an abortion so I could move on with my life, graduate from school, and do the right thing. I was also hurt because I'd gotten a letter in the mail to become a model, a teenage model. You couldn't be pregnant of course. There went my career out the window because I modeled when I was even younger, modeling clothing at Kmart and at a couple of other places (and I took ballet, tap, and aerobics). Then Mom tried to send me to one of those teen-pregnancy groups. But my future mother-in-law, who was Catholic and didn't believe in abortion, told me if I didn't marry her son that I couldn't ever see him again. So I refused to have the abortion, but it's just hurt me in the long run. I mean I wouldn't change anything now for the world. I love my children, and I have two beautiful grandchildren. But I wish sometimes I could go back and sort of redo a few things. I would have graduated high school and went to college and got a career. I did go back and get my GED. When you are at that age and people are telling you to "do *this*" or "if you don't do *this*, you can't see this person," your brain is just going in different directions. And it's hard to make the right decision. Being just a teenager, I didn't really know what was the best thing to do.

We had a courthouse wedding. My mom did not want to sign the papers, but she did, although she did not go to the courthouse with us. Actually it was just Jake and I. We didn't even have a witness with us—someone who was inside the courthouse was our witness. The priest of Jake's church would not marry us because I was already pregnant, and they don't believe in that unless you grew up in the Catholic religion. And the preacher at my church was going to marry us, but we ended up just going to the courthouse and doing that alone.

I was only fifteen, and I didn't even know Jake for five months before we were married. He was sixteen. I was a stupid, young, naïve girl. My sisters and brothers, all my family was very upset with me. I was leaving my mother, which broke her heart. And I moved in with Jake and his family, eleven people in the household—that was a lot in one house. Somehow we stayed married for thirteen years and had three children before I finally left him for good.

Jake was violent, but I didn't know that when we married. We stayed in a back bedroom of the house. On the wall he had hanging a bunch of posters; and when I took some down, there were probably fifteen holes in the wall that he had made with his fists. And even though I was pregnant, he would do wrestling moves on me. I was very lucky he didn't cause me to abort my child. And he beat on me about every day. I had to be careful about what I said, how I said it, how I walked, how I talked, and how I acted toward other people. My mother raised me to be an affectionate person and to respect my elders and just people in general. At church my mother taught me to be friendly, to be nice. I would go up and shake people's hand. If I knew them well enough, I'd give them a hug, just to be nice. But in my husband's eyes that was a no-no. I could not show affection in public. That was an absolute disgrace on him, to show affection. And in public we couldn't hold hands, I couldn't put my arms around him, I couldn't give him a kiss even on the cheek—no affection whatsoever.

Everyone in the household worked, except for me because I was pregnant. So I would cook and clean and have supper on the table and ready to go when everyone got home. Even for the children when they got off the school bus, I had snacks for them. I'd also get up in the morning and cook breakfast. It was like I was a maid pretty much the whole time I was there. I did end up getting a job when I was sixteen. I was taken to work and picked up at work. I was isolated and restricted to the household. I didn't have the friends I did have. They weren't allowed to come around, or I wasn't allowed to go around them. When Jake was playing with his band, I was not allowed to go, just every once in a while. And when I did go, I just had to sit there. I wasn't allowed to talk to nobody or shake hands or be friendly. I just had to sit there and keep quiet and do what he said. If I didn't, there were consequences when we got home. As I got older, I kinda started fighting back, I guess, rebelling.

It's not easy to get out of a situation like that. A lot of people think you should just leave. But it takes counseling, someone to go to that can help you through that process. And when someone's threatening your life or threatens you in some way, those threats run through your head and keep you staying in that relationship. My mother finally moved away to Florida. She had her own apartment, and I could have left and gone there at any time. But my mom says I was mentally manipulated to the point where I believed everything they said and nothing she said. And that infuriated my mother. "Why are you believing him over your own mother?"

Finally after two and a-half years into our marriage, I left him for almost five and a-half months. I moved in with my mother, working and taking care of my baby. During that time, Jake was staying with three women in an apartment, with three women doing cocaine. We filed for a divorce. His mother was really against us getting a divorce, whereas my mom wanted us to. He ended up coming to me, wanting me back. He got down on his hands and knees and begged me. My mom said, "You're crazy, please don't go, please don't go." And we had actually filed for divorce, and both of us had paid our money. It was to be set in stone. But he said he would never hurt me again. And at the time, we had one child; so I went back with him because I really truly loved him. He was my life. And we got back together. But it turned out we just wasted all that money, because he wanted us to stay together—but what he really wanted was us to stay together in an open relationship.

Everything was fine for about a year, and then the beatings started back up again. And I found out the way he is, though he's still not open with it—he's bisexual. And I didn't know that until about three years into our marriage or a little over. He kept it hidden from me. And that's a hard thing to handle when you're married to someone. If he had just been upfront and honest with me, we could have both worked it out. And this is the weird part: Jake had a nephew by adoption that was a few years older than us, and he was our first time with a male—Jake's nephew! To see him go down on another man was just really disgusting. I didn't know it, but they were doing it before Jake approached me about it. They were doing it behind my back, and then they approached me. Even pictures were took by Polaroids. We had Polaroids. I'd never done stuff like that in my life. Then to be approached and talked to about it, and Jake to tell me I didn't have a choice and that it was gonna get done whether I wanted to or not—that was just really weird.

And something else happened that I didn't think anything about being wrong at the time. I was young, and I thought Jake would be fine with it. What happened was,

Jake went out of town and left his nephew with me. While Jake was gone, his nephew and I done something. And Jake got mad because he somehow seen us. Oh, that didn't go over! I didn't think it was wrong because we'd already done something before, and I thought it was okay. It wasn't okay, it was not okay at all—it was horrible!

Before his nephew, I had not seen Jake with another man or participated with him. I had seen him with another woman as I mentioned earlier—doing the silly things with my girlfriend that Jake and I were doing when we were dating, things like going swimming naked at night and having sex in a backyard swimming pool. But later on he and her were messing around behind my back and going to a local motel—and they talked me into joining them in the motel. That really tore me up, seeing him and her having sex, seeing the man I married and loved having sex with another woman. And Jake continued the threesome stuff with the two of us, off and on for years. I hated it, but I did it because he wanted me to. There were other times Jake had sex with her, like even right after I had my baby and had just come home from the hospital. She called me on the phone and told me, "Jake just left here and we had sex." She always wanted to marry him, and I wish it had gone that way, to be honest. But the relationship with Jake and her finally pretty much fizzled out, and she went on to marry a couple of times. And way on down the road, Jake got two gentlemen, and we ended up doing a foursome. That only happened one time.

And I'm not perfect, no one is perfect, everyone makes mistakes. And I've did a lot of things. There were other times I was forced by him to have relationships with women along with him, and all that sort of thing. Sometimes we'd bring home men—*we* would, had to. It was for him, not me. It's not fun when you're forced to do it. If you weren't forced to do it, it might be enjoyable; but when you're forced to do it, it's not. I would go into the bathroom and cry. No one would believe the times I've ran out of the room, just bawling my eyes out—a lot. I hated it. It was awful. I hated doing it too because of diseases and stuff out there. I just thank the Lord that I never got anything. That scared me to death. I've kinda blocked that part out. I'd get so drunk—I would have to get so drunk, I mean plastered—to do that. So a lot of times I don't remember what happened or went on, but I was going to pretend. He'd just threaten me: if you don't do this, you're gonna regret it when we get home. Nothing was ever done to me in public.

It just hurt to see someone you truly love with someone else. Why would they want to do that if they truly love you? You should be happy in your marriage, you shouldn't be sad. But I was sad, very sad. And there were a lot of things, sexualwise, that are just really . . . it's almost disgusting to discuss and talk about some of the things. It turns your stomach. And he forced me to do other weird things, like he would hold me down and take razor blades and cut himself and cut myself, and we'd have to both eat each other's blood. Yeah, it was crazy. And if I even brought up the thought of leaving him at that point, he'd threaten to kill himself. It was horrible.

When you care and make love with someone, you just don't like doing that stuff. It turned him on, I guess. I don't think it was fun and games. It's just, that was what he wanted. It's his sex drive or whatever; and that's what he enjoyed doing. Later on I come to find out (when he was travelling on the road and I was sending him money to survive, because he said they weren't making enough money to eat and stuff) that actually he was taking the money I was sending him—and I was working two jobs—for prostitutes, drugs, and whatever.

When you are in an abusive relationship, some people think you can just walk out of it, but you can't. You see these TV shows, and they say, "If you're being abused or in neglect, call this number, and we'll help you." It's just not that simple, especially if you love that person or if you care for that person and you want to be there for them and help them. It's really hard to walk away from somebody. It's also hard to explain. I'm a caring person, or I try to care. And you don't want to do anything to hurt a person you really care about, even though they're hurting you, even if you give them leeway to straighten up and they won't. It's hard. That was the situation during the open marriage for pretty much the rest of our being together—thirteen years married—so off and on for ten more years. But all that stuff wasn't constant, it was just every once in a while, although I would have to say no a lot—then he would get really mad. I just couldn't handle it. I'm just not that type of person.

Even when I was doing what he wanted me to do, he cheated behind my back. I didn't know how bad it was until after I divorced him, and all his friends come up and told me everything. One friend was telling me that when

Jake was on the road travelling, he would have a prostitute, and his friend would film them. I didn't know none of this. Sometimes he wouldn't let me go to the bar where they would be playing, and we'd get in a argument over it. But other times he'd let me go, the next night or something; and I'd be actually sitting with the girl, talking to her, that he had had sex with the night before. It ran through my head that I would just override it and go on. I shouldn't have, but I did, because you do anything to make the one you love happy, I guess. Just let things go, and that's what I did. But there's a point in time I had to stop, and that's when I got pregnant with my last son. Jake hit me in the stomach and tried to smother me to get me to abort my child. Yeah, that's when I took off. He had pulled all the phone wires out of the wall—cell phones had just started coming out—so I had no way to contact anybody. And I didn't have a vehicle—they wouldn't let me have a vehicle. That was another way of controlling me and to keep up with where I was and what I was doing. For both of my jobs, I'd have to get my employer's permission for either my husband, my ex-mother-in-law, or my ex-father-in-law to pick up my check. I never seen a paycheck. I'm serious, I never seen a paycheck, either one of my jobs. Since I was waitressing, I got paid in tips too, so I would try to hide money, cash. But he would always find it. I couldn't hide it anywhere he didn't find it. I was never able to save or put away money. The only way I was able to do it was if I gave it to my mother. My ex-mother-in-law would say, "Well, give it to me, and I'll take it and save it for you. But that didn't happen. I'd give it to her, and if Jake got to a point where he said he had to have it, she'd give it to him.

He was involved with other women; but I couldn't've been involved with someone even if I had wanted to, which I didn't. He knew every move I made. I had no freedom, none. And that's when I became an alcoholic. He gave me the drink—and the beatings. I never got any broken bones, just beatings. At a couple of waitressing jobs, I'd go in; and my boss would have to pull me aside and get her makeup out and try to cover the bruises up on my neck or my face, because she said I can't go waiting tables with bruises on my body. And two times Jake busted the back of my head. Once on the headboard in the bedroom, he hit my head against it until my head bust open. And then in the bathroom, there's a soap dish attached to the wall. He pushed me down on that, and it busted my head open. My ex-mother-in-law was there in the house, and she wouldn't take me to the ER. She said, "Just get in the shower." I can remember the blood coming down onto the shower floor both times. She'd just say, "Don't call the law. I'll go light a candle for you at St. Mary's." She was an RN, a registered nurse, and she just put Steri-Strips on it and said, "It'll be okay, it'll be fine." But I don't think I really was. I think I had a little bit of a concussion. Any time you get your head busted open, there's a chance of concussion. The last guy I was with, he hated touching my head because he said I got indentions, "I guess it's where you gotten hit." I said, "I don't know."

I never did call the law on Jake while we were married, so I was never able to prove he was abusive to me or my children. But he never stopped. Later toward the end when we were living in a trailer down the road from his mother's, my second son, only four or five years old, would call out, "Mommy, why is the trailer shaking, what's that noise?" And it was because Jake and I would be at one end and the kids be in bed at the other end, and Jake would be hitting me. He would also come home drunk at three or four o'clock in the morning and make me get up and cook his meals. If his steak wasn't cooked right or something, he would throw his plate with all the food up against the wall.

Most of the time I was married to him, I worked while he traveled on the road with his band. I stayed home to take care of the kids and work my jobs. He even went to college for a short time while I was married to him, but I don't think he even finished a semester. I know we ran up a credit-card bill of almost ten thousand dollars, which I think might have been from some of the college expenses. That was near the end of the marriage. Also when I would move us out into an apartment or somewhere, he always wanted to come back to his parents' house. We could never be out on our own. It was just impossible. I mean, I tried to make it work. He wanted to be at his mother's home. He was dependent on her. And after our divorce he lived with his mother for sixteen years.

In Jake's parents' home, they always kept alcohol, but when we were living in the trailer, I would hide it. Either my mother-in-law or brother-in-law would let me stop by a liquor store, and I'd buy me a little pint or half a pint, which I kept in my purse or would hide in the trailer. If he would find it, he would dump it out or take it for hisself. He was an alcoholic too; we both were. I wouldn't touch the floor in the morning till I had a swig of vodka, straight out of my purse, hot. It was an everyday thing. I could drink a whole fifth—it wouldn't bother me—and I often did. Oh yeah, I could outdrink him, seriously; and that would make him mad at me. I wadn't trying to outdrink him, I could just drink and hold my alcohol. He's a big man, six-foot-two and weighed 275 pounds, but I could outdrink him. He might have been doing more than just drinking is the reason I could. I had been drinking like that probably about five or six years toward the end, but when I found out I was pregnant with my third child, believe it or not, I put it down. And that's when I left him because, as I said, he tried to abort the child. He said the child wasn't his, that I was cheating on him. But I wasn't. The kids were in school. I didn't have a vehicle to go get them, so I took off on foot, almost six months into my third pregnancy, and walked to a medical center where my mom was having a stent put in.

It wasn't long after leaving Jake I met a fellow in a bar that was the first person who would have anything to do with me. And I married him—within three months of our relationship. I rebounded, I guess. I'd been with the same man for thirteen years—I didn't know how to be single. He was four years younger; but we just connected, and I enjoyed being with him. He had a really good job, working at a local factory, and had been there for ten years when they shut the doors. We were living in a trailer on a farm about fifteen miles out from where I had been living. His family would bring untamed horses, and he had a fenced-in lot where he trained the horses to sell. He liked to bass fish professionally and hunt bear and turkey, stuff like that. He had two boys by his previous marriage, and I had the three boys by mine. And although all my boys weren't living with us, they were coming over; so sometimes we'd have all five at one time. He was good to me and he was good to my children. He was a really nice guy. I just wasn't in love with him.

I had a great job working for a corporation making hotel reservations, but I hurt my back exercising. I was really overweight and was exercising with one of those little rolling wheels on a bar. I think that's what caused me having issues with my sciatica and degenerative disc disease. Anyway, they ended up putting me on short-term disability for almost two years. I was only twenty-eight years old, but I was walking with a cane and couldn't jog or exercise. It was horrible. They wanted to do surgery, but I heard a lot of bad things about back surgery. So I refused when the doctor wanted me to have it done. I think hurting my back also hurt our marriage. I kind of went downhill on him.

My money went into his checking account, and we always had money in the bank. He was good with money and wasn't greedy or nothing, just very conservative—he just didn't like to spend money. He let the trailer get in very bad shape, especially the bathrooms and the water pipes. He just wouldn't fix things. There were mice holes and mice coming up on the couch. And I even had a couple of cats in the house, but they didn't seem to want to kill the mice.

I only lived with him for two and a-half years before a girlfriend of mine came and, seeing the condition of the trailer, said, "You're not living like this; I'm getting you out of here." She made me pack up what I could and took me out of there. She just couldn't accept that I was living in a place in that kind of shape with my two-year-old child. So I left my husband and divorced him, even though it would be a year and a half before the divorce was finalized. He was a wonderful man, and we never had one argument. To be honest, I probably made a mistake leaving him.

After I left, I stayed with my girlfriend for several months and met a guy there that was at first interested in her. But she didn't like him and even warned me not to have anything to do with him. However, I did; and we started living together in his parents' basement. He had done some time in prison—I didn't know anything about it until a couple of years down the road. But he and I were together almost six years. I had never been treated so good in my whole life. He put me up on a pedestal. He'd bring me a flower or a candy bar or music box or something home every day—I mean something every day, the whole five years we were together. And I'd never had that before.

He got me into what is called dumpster diving. We would get stuff out of dumpsters, clean it up, take it to a flea market, and make money. We mainly went behind big department stores that throw away stuff that may have a rip in it or something, but nothing really wrong with it. They just couldn't sell it, and they would throw it in the dumpster. We would go, maybe twelve, one o'clock in the morning to the dumpsters and dig stuff out. But he was just mischief, mischief, and like, staying in trouble. He was a very hyper person. He always had to be doing something, and I think he just enjoyed doing illegal things like stealing and stuff like that. He would steal anything, everything. Why, he'd disappear in the middle of the night while I was in bed, and I'd wake up the next morning with stuff in the room that I would have no idea where it came from. One time there was a large object all covered up in the corner. It was a settee. I asked, "Where did you get this from?" And he said, "None of your business." He stole golf carts off golf courses and all kinds of stuff.

Dumpster diving was one thing; but him doing that, I just did not like. We both had good jobs. He was a landscaper, and I was a supervisor at a telemarketing firm. It's not like we needed the money. I don't know—stealing to him was like an adrenalin rush, I guess. He got caught; and if it wouldn't have been for me, he would have been put back in prison. Since I was making decent money at that time, I was able to get a good lawyer and get him placed on house arrest. However, he violated his parole several times. They would come to the house, just pop in; and if he wasn't there, he'd be "violated." The first time he did thirty days; the second time he did fifty-four days. It got old, and I stayed stressed-out living with him.

As I said, he did treat me like a queen, but I was to pay for it. The main way was that Jake used my living with him to take my son away from me. I didn't know it, but in the state of Tennessee you can't live with a child by another person in the home of a felon unless you are married to him. Okay, the judge wouldn't allow me to get a divorce while I was pregnant because he said the child would be considered a bastard. Then five years after my first divorce, Jake (even though he had denied that he was the father) took my son from me on the basis I was illegally living with a convicted felon.

The date he took my child was November 7, 2005. I'll never forget it because I had my son in day care, and I couldn't even go pick him up because of a court order. I couldn't even see him that day. Jake went and took him out of day care and took him out of preschool. (He had already got custody of my two other boys for abandonment after I walked out from him.) At that point everything got really bad. The guy I was with, the felon, his father ended up having terminal cancer. And I'd started up my drinking again. When I'd get off work, I'd get me some airplane bottles and drink about four of them before I went home. I'd be drunk when I walked in the house. One day when I got home, his father was laying there dead. It was awful. We got in a big ol' argument and ended breaking up. All this happened—I lost my son, he lost his father, and we broke up—all within like a three-, four-month period. And come to find out, he never truly loved me, I don't think any man that's been with me ever truly loved me. I always just picked the wrong man.

After Jake took my youngest son, I began to fight to regain my children. I would hire a lawyer, but Jake would always hire a better lawyer or outdo me in some way. I had no control, and it turned out to be just awful, because he ended up taking his anger out on the children. He was mean to the kids, and I didn't find this out until this past year.

Finally I moved in with my niece, my sister's daughter, for a few months. Then I moved to a small city in Virginia, where I started working as a manager of a burrito shop. I started dating a gentleman for about two years. He had a farm and also built those big ol' machines that went into the coal mines. I quit drinking. I just woke up one day, and alcohol started turning my stomach every time I smelt beer, wine, or liquor. I mean just the smell of it or even thinking about it. I quit. Honestly, I just started drinking a little bit this past month or so, and that's been the first after eleven years.

My mom fell ill, and I moved to be with her, back to the homeplace where she was now living. She needed help with her sister, Aunt Lou, the one that was mean to me and my mother. So I ended up taking care of even her! My mother had it rough. She did a lot of taking care of her family members and always ended up getting hurt in the end. Before I moved back to Tennessee to be with my mother, things had been going well with the gentleman I was dating. We were getting along great. He had a great son, but a daughter that was not so great. She stole from stores and stuff. Then she ended up pregnant. He was putting all his effort into her and his soon-to-be grandchild. I don't blame him for that. I mean you should always pick your family over a person that you're dating or whatever. So our relationship ended, I think, because of all that. Anyway, my mom needed my help, and I had to go. What really hurt is that the gentleman

I was dating said he didn't have nothing in Tennessee, so there was no reason for him to come visit.

When my aunt passed away, Mom and I moved into an apartment in a neighboring city. During that process, I dated this guy I met when I was working as a cashier at a gas station. That was in 2008. He lived with my mother and I until he broke up with me for a period in 2012, the year my mother died. He left for another woman, a younger woman in her twenties that had three children. It just tore me all to pieces. Even before Mom died, it was really rough for me, trying to take care of her, seeing her dwindle away and her wanting to die. She had diabetes, heart disease, neuropathy, just a lot of health issues in general. With all that stress, depression, and personal issues, I ended up having a nervous breakdown. I tried to kill myself. It was stupid of me for doing what I'd done—slit my wrist. My mom called 911. The police showed up, and they made me go with them in the back of a cruiser to the hospital, where I was for hours. Then the police took me from there straight to a psychiatric hospital. The first day I was there, I threw an awful fit; and they almost shot me up with lithium because I was screaming and kicking—yeah. No one was at home to take care of my mother or my dog. I didn't know what was gonna happen to my mom. I wanted out. The people at the psychiatric hospital said, "If you want to get out, you need to do this, this, and this." I's like—"Okay." So I did what they told me, and I got out in five days.

My brothers and sisters intervened about my mother when I got out of the hospital. They come and took her away from me and take her to a nursing home in Winston-Salem, North Carolina. My mom was prejudiced, and they put her in a nursing home that was 90 percent black. She was one of only two white persons in there, and she died within six months. They took her away from me, and I didn't get to finish taking care of her. I only got to see her twice while she was in Winston-Salem. And the day before she died, she couldn't even speak. She had pneumonia, and she wasn't able to even talk with me on the phone. And I told her, "Mom," I said, "it's okay if you want to go—go ahead and go. Don't be miserable, don't wait on me. I'll get to Winston-Salem as soon as I can." I said, "If you want to go, go." Nine o'clock that morning they called and told me she'd passed away the hour before. I had taken care of her for six years, but I didn't get to finish taking care of her. And the other family members didn't even want her.

The apartment was in my name in case something happened to my mom, so I'd have a roof over my head. But I had a hard time finding a job, and the guy who had lived with us and helped with the bills wouldn't help me. I couldn't afford to pay for the apartment, so I ended up getting kicked out and being homeless.

I was out on the street. Not easy. Panhandled for money. Not fun. I was around a bunch of homeless people that were crackheads and meth heads, and it's scary. I don't do meth. My teeth problems are from when I was a child. I stayed in and out of the hospital, and I had ear infections—I almost went deaf. I always kept walking pneumonia and took a lot of antibiotics. I was told that if I don't keep going to a dentist on a regular basis that my teeth, which were really fine, would probably end up being what they are now. I have not been to a dentist in over sixteen years, and before that I hadn't been to one since before I got married. My teeth problems now are just from years of not taking care of my teeth.

I wasn't on the street for very long, only four—not even four—months. I'd met people that had been out there for years. I met a guy named Tennessee. He's almost seventy years old. He was an alcoholic. Some of the people are homeless because they've had issues—a lot of them are drug addicts, alcoholics, and veterans. Tennessee was a veteran. I was walking ten to twelve miles a day, and I lost forty pounds in one month, just eating ramen noodles and drinking a lot of water and cutting out sodas. I was trying to find a job so I could get on my feet, but it's kind of hard to find a job if you don't have a vehicle. Mainly I stayed at night with people I knew. I found out that a couple of the girls I stayed with—I'd went to high school with—were no longer friends after thirty-some years because they had issues, like one of them was on needle dope so bad I didn't even stay with her four days. She told me she was clean, but she's not, still on needle dope. But I usually had a roof over my head every night. That is thanks to people that I know out there. One of my friends . . . she takes in homeless people, and that's how she pays back to her community.

Some of the people on the street that had money probably went out and had sex—that's how they got money. But I've refused. I got propositioned, and I just couldn't do that, can't do that, won't do that. That's not me. Going through what I went through in a relationship with my marriage and the way I was treated, I just can't do that. I get too paranoid, too worried about situations like that. I would just panhandle for change. Some people would cuss me out, tell me to get a job. Some people would be nice to me and give me some money.

I got off the streets when that guy who left me for the younger woman took me back in. He did have that other woman, but far as that goes, he never had anybody else. He said he can't handle me being out on the streets and he wouldn't kick me out again, wouldn't let me be homeless again. He lived in a little bitty, one-bedroom apartment; and I moved into it with him. Then later in 2013 or 2014 he had an apartment in an adjacent city, and I moved in with him there. We lived there only about six or seven months, and then we moved into a trailer. He's on disability, but every once in a while he'd do a concrete job "under the table." I got down to 103 pounds. I started working in a little restaurant, deli-type place. Then from there I worked at Kentucky Fried Chicken. We were living together as friends, not lovers; and our relationship really went on for about eight years, off and on. We just fell apart, but I did care about him. It's been a rough four years. He would want me, but then he wouldn't want me around, then he'd want me around again. He just flip-flopped. He also had his own personal issues to deal with. I can't really explain. He was having male issues, and he wouldn't go to a doctor. So we were just friends. He cared for me, and I cared for him; but we weren't really active, and it bothered him that we couldn't be. He moved to Virginia Beach, and he just let me stay in his trailer a while. That lasted until a little over two and a-half months ago. Then he told me to pack my stuff and find somewhere to go. It's just that we weren't meant to be together. We're still friends. In fact, he's just recently called me.

After I moved out—would anybody believe?—I moved into the same house I first lived in with Jake and his parents. I was living there to take care of my ex-mother-in-law. She lived there with June, my ex-sister-in-law, my youngest sixteen-old son (that I still don't have custody of and that has lived there since he was five years old), and my middle twenty-four-old son (that moved into an apartment with a friend not long after I moved in). All my children have been raised in that house. My oldest son is married and lives in the same vicinity. Jake got kicked out of his parents' house about six months ago for elder abuse, abusing his mother. Jake's family once had money, but he broke them, borrowing it. He remarried once, somebody we grew up with—but not my old girlfriend that he was messing around with when we were married. He and his wife had a child, but he gave up his parental rights for it.

All these years he wouldn't let me see my kids, threatened to throw me in jail, threatened all this stuff—and then after all that, I was back in my children's life. Really, for the first time in sixteen years! My ex-mother-in-law was the one that wanted me in her house and who asked her other children if I could stay so she wouldn't be by herself. When I first moved in, she said she was going to hell. And I said,

"Why you want to go to hell for?" And she said, "All the things that have happened in this family all these years." And I looked at her, and I said, "God forgives. People don't forgive, but God forgives. Things happen." Strange things do happen. There I was in that house which is only about a mile from the trailer where her son and I lived when I left him.

While I was taking care of my ex-mother-in-law, I was trying to concentrate on myself and my children. But I was also having a lot of issues with my kids being angry with me. And I was still flustered, not at ease with anything. And I won't be at ease until I know I'm stable, stable jobwise—roof over my own head without somebody supplying it for me. But it's hard to be at ease until I can be at ease with myself. I can't blame nobody but myself for the situation I'm in. It's my own doing. I've got to get myself fixed—just as simple as that. I done this to myself, I can get myself out of it. But while I was back there in that house, I was a little more at ease because I got to see my children more, especially my sixteen-year-old. That made me feel good. I love that.

And things went pretty well for a short time, taking care of my former mother-in-law; but I knew that it wasn't gonna last. For one thing, June was holding a grudge against her mother. She told me, even in front of her mother, how mean her mother had been to her and the other kids when they were growing up. I didn't realize how bad it was. I knew my ex-mother-in-law was a foster parent for fifty years and took in foster children—and that Jake, June, and one of the other siblings were adopted. But I didn't know she used to tie the children to the bed, ankle to the bed, and also lock them out of the house during the day until she was ready for them to come in. And I had no idea that she used to call her daughter a slut, a whore, and a good-for-nothing piece of crap. I knew none of that. (It does make me sort of understand why Jake was the way he was toward me—because of the way he was treated.) When June was bringing up all this stuff, it really upset her mother. And June just looked at her mother and said, "It hurts to hear the truth, doesn't it?" And her mother told her to go fuck herself. I had no trouble with my ex-mother-in-law while I was taking care of her, but June in less than three months kicked me out.

Again I had to depend upon another girlfriend—this time Irene. I have known her for a long time, and she was living on a temporary basis in a trailer that belonged to a male friend of hers that was in the county jail at the time. She helped me move into the trailer with some of my stuff that was stored in the basement of my ex-mother-in-law's house.

Irene is the same age as me, forty-five, and has been married three or four times. She comes from a big family— her mother had ten children. And Irene has three children, one by one man and one by another—the other child I'm not sure of. I try not to pry into everybody's business. We went to school together, and she was shy, just like me, quiet. We weren't popular and kept to ourselves. But her parents made her quit hanging out with me when I got pregnant. It's just been the past few years that I started hanging out with her again. She is divorced and has gone through a lot.

She and I had some wild times back in the days, but we're grown up now. We went out together partying a few times during the several months before I moved in with her, but she's been partying way too much with others for some time.

One of the nights we went out partying, we were drinking a lot of alcohol and ended up at Bud's. He has a bar built in his basement called the Man Cave where his friends are always dropping in for some beers. We were drunk that night, and this is what happened. While we were there drinking, a man and his twenty-one-year-old son came in. I don't remember exactly what was going on at first, but Irene started it by asking about the son. The son didn't want anything to do with her and got madder than heck. She was sitting on this big table, then just laying back on it. All of a sudden, the man jumped on top of Irene, and they had it right there on the table. I didn't have anything to do with that, but they wanted me to do my "little thing," so I did. And Irene said, "Okay, it's your turn, it's your turn." I said, "No, no, no, no." Anyway, she and that man pulled me up on the table. He held me down, and she pulled my pants off and did "that" to me. That didn't bother me, but I was getting ready to get up, and the man just jumped in on me. I was up and got him off me in about fifteen seconds, because that wasn't . . . I didn't like that . . . yeah, that bothered me. As soon as she had got up off of me . . . I mean I was getting up . . . and it was just like . . . I mean he literally jumped . . . and I got up and he quit. I mean that was just "unh-ah"—I did not like that at all. That really pissed me off, but I just let it be. I just don't want to argue and fight. It ended up being a bad night.

Then there was a second bad night that started at Bud's. Irene and me had some drinks with another girl, Vickie, at Vickie's house. We were just gonna hang out there, but these two other girls showed up. One was on needle dope, and the other one used to be a prostitute, I think. (Those two partied for about two weeks, and men were just coming in and out of where they were staying.) Anyway, they wanted to go out with us partying. So we left and went by Bud's. After we were there a little while, we started acting a little crazy and kissing each other, teasing the guys. It was playing—that's all it was, playing. We didn't go any farther than that. We don't. It's playing, it's to tease the men. I think a lot of women do it. Almost every woman out there has a girlfriend, and when they go out on the town or something . . . I don't know . . . I can't speak for everyone . . . but there are a lot of women out there that will dress up provocative and go out to have a good time; and if men are looking at them or something, they'll do their little kissing each other like a lesbian thing, just to tease the men, just making men want you more, I guess. I don't know why—it's funny—men like to see two women kissing or smacking each other's ass or dancing provocative. Back in the day when we'd go out, that was our plan, was to tease the men in that way, tease them, and just have fun. Every once in a while, one of us would get a man, and the other one would go home without one. I just think, it's playful fun, it's not hurting no one. Maybe it is, but for my part, I don't think it is. For us girls now, the single wives, we're older now, so we don't really do much of the bar scenes anymore; but we still like to hang out and have a good time. We like to dance—I like to dance. And if there's men around, we are gonna tease, make the men jealous. I don't know if it's an instinct in women or what, but it seems like every woman I've ever hung around with, it's like, "Let's do this, make that man jealous." Especially if they like someone, just to see the reaction on the man's face. Conniving—women are conniving. But as far as anything else, most of the time it don't go any farther than that. When women drink a lot and there's men around, sometimes they're a little off-the-wall crazy. They like to play.

To be honest, Irene and I have done a lot of experimentation together. Sometimes things just happen, and sometimes you just go with the flow, especially if you've been drinking a lot. Now, Irene used not to drink. She is a little bit crazy and wild—like she is now—just since her mother died and her man left her. He was twenty years younger than her. She said she just couldn't get her life back. And she said her father wouldn't let her stay at home, so she goes from place to place. She was always calling me on the phone with something wrong or going wrong or she's upset. Just like me, I swim on the crazy side. Anyway, that's when she started drinking a lot and being crazy.

Now, Irene was doing some other pretty wild things that second night at Bud's. She wanted to take the padding out of the bra that was sewn into the dress she was wearing that Vickie gave her. One of the guys there said, "Just pull it down and take it out." So Irene pulled the top of the dress down, and everyone helped her get the padding out. And Irene loves sex, a little bit too much. It's just ridiculous. She tried to get me to do all kinds of things here recently, like threesomes, but I said no. Back in the day, yeah, we did a lot of crazy things. But while we were at Bud's, I do think there was a little competition going on between Vickie and Irene towards me. Anyway Vickie said to Irene something like, "I love you"; and Irene said, "I'll just turn lesbian." Vickie replied, "Well, you and I will get together." Then Vickie turned to me and said, "What do you think about that?" And I said, "Go for it." That made Vickie mad, jealous, or something.

Okay, me myself, to be honest, I have went the other way and dated a woman. I ended up doing all the work—she didn't do nothing. She'd never done it before, and I went down on her, but she never once went down on me. I did it all. So that's that. It just can't go one way, it has to go both ways. Also she got mean towards me. She'd hit me and stuff. I can't take that no more. I think she liked the roughhousing, and I'm not like that. Unh-ah, no! And she brought men home when we used to go out. And if she didn't want to sleep with them, she'd say, "I don't want to have sex with him, come sleep in the bed with us." She would put them in the middle, and we'd take a sleep. However, he wouldn't sleep all night long because it was nerve-racking for him. And I wouldn't touch the guy—that would be interfering on her turf, and I wouldn't do that. But if she wanted to have sex with them, then I slept on the couch. It happened a lot. I think she took me out because she knew they would be attracted to her and not me. I was a pretty big girl at the time, almost two hundred pounds. I'm not anymore, but at the time I was. She knew she would get the men and I wouldn't. That's pretty much what it boiled down to. But after she was abusive to me, everything ended very quickly.

Anyway, at Bud's that second bad night, we kept doing crazy stuff and finally left and went to a bar. Things got worse there. The two other girls with us were accused of stealing money from one of the customers, and they were thrown out of the bar. One of them said Irene and me were doing tricks for money in the men's room—which was definitely a lie. After the two girls were thrown out, they wanted to go to a fast food place, get something to eat, and wait for a friend there—for some drugs, I'm sure. Irene and me ended back at Vickie's. And things were okay, after I cooked something to eat, until Vickie started cutting down my children and me. That's when I just go and grab up my things, and Irene and me left.

There was also a third night at Bud's that was a little crazy. That time it all started again at Vickie's, drinking. Vickie doesn't know how to socially drink. She just wants to drink to be drunk, and that's all she really cares about, is getting drunk. But she wanted to go to Bud's, so we went to Bud's. We drank some more there, and Bud was saying to another man something about some woman who showed her boobs to somebody for twenty-five dollars. Vickie said, "I'd show mine for twenty-five dollars." And this other guy reached in his wallet and pulled out twenty-five dollars.

Vickie started taking off her shirt and bra, so I did too. Bud pulled out another twenty-five for me and got me to show my "kitty-cat" too. It embarrassed me, but I needed the money. I was broke. That's horrible to say, but that's the truth. The only reason I did it was for the money. Otherwise I wouldn't have done it. But I must admit, another time at Bud's I did try to get Vickie to pull her bra down on the count of three just to be teasing—although neither one of us actually did, that time. Maybe I was going to flatter the men—showing them a little bit of skin from a woman might make them feel better. I don't know, I really don't know. I don't do stuff like that unless I get drunk. When I drink, the more apt and easier it is to do crazy things. Alcohol makes you do a lot of things easier. Fill the alcohol in me, and I'll do crazy things; but I won't go to extremes. I might pull down my bra or tease—that's it. I'm not like Irene and do a "BJ." I'll take that back, I don't know. It would just depend on the situation and who was involved. That's all I can say about that. I don't know how else to explain it.

Once, however, I did try out—that was also when I was heavier, about 185—I did try to get a job in a nudie bar, a strip club, dancing. And I can dance. But the thing was, I think, I was too embarrassed of my body, too ashamed to show it out there on the dance floor in front of a bunch of people, to get the job. I can't explain it, but just the way I presented myself was horrible. I'm not heavy now, and I'm not as embarrassed as I used to be; but in certain areas of my body, I am. I think Vickie feels the same about her body. She has a very attractive body, and men really go for her. But she hates her body. She complains about it all the time. I think she knows she's pretty, but she just downgrades herself. She says she's ugly, this and that—she says she's gained weight or something. I think it comes from lack of self-esteem—makes me think about myself. But for years she's just been wanting someone to love her and settle down with her. That's all she wants. I told her, "Just don't rush it, it'll come to you." She says she wants that; but if she got it, I wonder, would she want to go back to the good times? I don't think so. Each time she's been married, she's gone into the housewife mode. She don't care about the drink or anything else, and she's happy in that relationship. I've seen it. She wants that housewife, a husband, be home cooking supper and taking care of him. That's what she wants, but that just hasn't happened yet—because she keeps picking the wrong men, just like I do. That's the truth.

Sometimes I look at my life, how I lived it; and I wonder how I've survived. I've been damaged of course. I've been diagnosed with PTSD because of some of the stuff in my life—that's what the doctors say. I don't know. I think everybody has a little bit of PTSD, but I just have to kinda take hold of my life in some way, shape, or form. In the long run, I think I've built up my self-esteem—to be myself and more confident in my life. I've learned a lot. Instead of having someone being over me, telling me what to do, I control my own life now. And to some extent I've recovered a lot from my relationships with men and hanging out with girlfriends. This last relationship with a man that I've had has really hurt me. It's my third serious relationship, and

I just don't know what to do about it—just give it up or keep trying or let it go for now and let it take care of itself? I don't want to die a lonely old woman like my mom did. But I feel I'm more confident than I've ever been about my appearance and about the way I talk and present myself. I'm more confident than I have ever been in my life. But it's took years for me to accomplish that. I have flashbacks and dreams—things I don't like, wish I wouldn't have done, but I have. There's nothing I can do about those things. I just have to take one day at a time and move forward, just do the best I can. Someone might think I feel sorry for myself all the time, but I blame myself for the mistakes I've made. And I don't guess that's feeling sorry for myself. We all have our issues to worry about, and mine is that I'm worrying about my children. Many a time I just want to give up, but you can't give up, you just got to keep going. I'm not gonna be stupid, like some people out here that's shot themselves, because what's that gonna solve? Nothing, you're dead. You can't fix something when you're dead, so there's no sense in killing yourself. And I want to be there for my children, but I need to get my stuff in order before I can even do that. It's frustrating. And I guess a lot of us are still wanting to find someone out there that would just really love us—find our mate. And that just hasn't happened for me yet.

Right now, I'm packing up to leave a friend's house with most of my stuff again, and go off with somebody that I have known for years. I hope it'll all work out. We'll see.

Going without a Target

Portrait: a white woman, born in 1968 to a middle-class family, who grew up in a small city (ca. 34,000 population). Her formal education includes a diploma from high school (ca. 2,000 enrollment) and classes in a university for part of a year. She is the mother of two daughters.

Notable Personae: father, mother, sister, girlfriends, husbands, children, "uncle," and male resident.

Themes (among others): dysfunctional family, religious background, patriotism, peer influence, effects of personal appearance, dating activity, employment, marital relationship, maternal instincts, child care, financial evolution, substance abuse, race, homicide, manufacture and sale of drugs, arrests and incarcerations, legal and moral issues, social services, resilience, "the good life," and personal philosophy.

My father was a senior officer in the army, my mom was an officer's wife, I have an older sister, and I'm the black sheep of the family for sure. They were good parents, great, great parents. We ate, drank, breathed everything "America"—it was a real patriotic family. And we went to church every time the doors were open, Baptist. Strict Southern Baptist Republicans, right-wing faith and beliefs—that's the family I came from. Daddy was in his nineties when he died with dementia. I was a big "daddy's girl." Me and my mom don't have the best relationship. It's kinda okay, but a little strained. She was forty-one when I was born in 1968, really from a different generation. She's kind of snobbish in a way, and I'm not. She's in her eighties now and still kicking in the house I grew up in. Daddy was fifty-two when I was born. That's when he decided to retire, come home, and go into the reserves. They had a lot of views that I thought, after I grew up, Well, damn, where am I going with this? Like they led me to believe that Martin Luther King was a bad man. I didn't know who King was, and why did they always talk down about him? Daddy also didn't believe in the Vietnam War, and they talked down about the Vietnam vets when they came back, about the way they acted, like they deserved something. Well, damn, they did deserve something. My family thought that there's always a black and a white, there's never a gray area. And I say there is usually always a gray area.

In high school I think I had like a D average. I mean, I was strictly there for the social life. I had a friend lived up the street and she had her own car and she drove us to school, you know. She would come and get us real early in the morning. And Mama would be like, "Why? Your school doesn't even start for an hour and a half." But we would go early to get high before school. We'd smoke pot, you know. We shared a friend who worked graveyard shift, and she was just getting off work as we were going to school. So we'd go to her house and get high and hang out. Then once we got high, we didn't want to go to school: "So we'll just go in late." Then later, "Well, let's just not go in at all." That was my junior and senior year. It wasn't so bad in the tenth grade; well, I's partying then, but my truancies and absences, you know, were in the eleventh and twelfth.

We did a lot of binge drinking. One time we were at a keg party up on a mountain road near a campground, and we're all tripping acid. The reserves were doing exercises up there that weekend; and all of a sudden, these military men came up near us and scared us to death. We thought we were crazy, you know. We thought we were hallucinating, seeing stuff. "Did you see that guy?" We were so scared because we were all underage and tripping acid and were gonna get into big trouble. But then we talked to them, and they were nice and walked on. We just sat there and laughed and laughed.

These habits of ours were a little expensive, so we'd do different things to get the money, like I'd tell my Daddy: "Daddy, I started my period, I need . . . " And that's about all I'd have to say, and he'd give me some money. And me and Lisa—she was my best friend and still is to this day—I can't believe we'd do this, but we panhandled. We'd ask people at school all day long, "Do you have twenty cents?" or "Do you have a dollar or more?" or whatever. Everybody'd give us a little change, and at the end of the day me and Lisa would have enough to get us a twelve-pack. That's what we'd do. We were stupid, we were so stupid. If my daughters knew the things I did, I would die. Sometimes we'd pull up beside of people in traffic, guys in pickup trucks or something, and we'd get their attention by sucking in our breath on a make-believe joint—people we didn't even know, and then we'd pull over right there and smoke a joint with them and drink. Crazy, crazy, crazy stuff.

We got away with a bunch. My parents, I think, were kinda tired by the time I came along, you know what I mean? And we were spoiled. I never got a spanking, ever, from my daddy. He tried to spank me when I was like seventeen, and I turned around and looked at him, "You should have tried that about fourteen years ago, and we wouldn't be standing here tonight." He just never spanked me, and they would maybe ground me for one night. But my sister—she's a huge overachiever—she really resented that, because she did get spankings.

I'd go out every night, just about every single night—not stay out late on school nights, just to maybe nine o'clock. Now if my daughter didn't come home from school from four till nine at night, I'd be upset. But often I might call my mom once when school got out and not talk with her again till I got home. And for the longest time—and I think all this is stupid—I remember my friends would get really mad at me, because as soon as I would hit the door when I came home at night, I'd go straight to the shower. And I'd go straight because Mom hated smoking. She'd always said if she caught me with a cigarette, she was gonna make me eat it. And she had a nose, she could smell anything. And I'd usually have a friend stay the night with me, and we'd be walking through my bedroom; but the next thing you'd know, I'd leave them there and be taking a shower. Daddy didn't really ever fuss at me for it, but he was in bed half the time by the time I came home anyway, because he had to work the next morning. He was over a unit out there at the Army Reserves. All told, he was in for about fifty years. He was a real hard-core soldier, no pansy, you know what I mean? He really should have had a boy, and I was the closest thing to a boy, because my sister, you know, she's a lot like Mama.

While I was in high school, we had a clique of eight girls, and we were always with one or more of the others. That was our pack, and they all still live in this area. I didn't do much dating until I was a senior, and I didn't really have a boyfriend until then. I was fat, not real fat, but I was chubby. But Lisa was a brazen whore back then, she was. But now, she's nothing at all like that; but when she was a teenager, yes, she was a little whore. I dated one guy, Brian, during my senior year, and we were together three years after that when we both went to college. He came from a dysfunctional family with an abusive alcoholic father. It was an awful situation, just awful. I'd never seen anything like it firsthand. I brought him home one night to show my folks how his father had beat the hell out of him. My parents were asleep when I came in, so I told my boyfriend to go get on the couch. Then I spoke out to my folks, "Okay, I'm home now, all right?" Mom came into the room to bitch me out for coming in so late, and she's like, "Why is he on the couch?" I said, "His daddy beat him up." She was like, "And, so?"—like, "It's not my problem." They were like that, whereas I'm entirely different—my teenage daughter's boyfriend lived with us. His mama is a raging bitch; and, yeah, I'd rather he'd live with me than live with that crazy, raging bitch.

With Brian I mainly drank. When I started dating him, I didn't smoke pot as much as I did when my girlfriend was coming to pick me up for school in the mornings. When her dad found out that she wasn't going to the public high school anymore, he took her car away, started her in a private school. And I had to find alternate rides to school. I wasn't gonna ride the bus with them geeks and losers, and I wasn't gonna ride in one of Dad's station wagons, you know what I mean? So I rode with one of my other girlfriends that was in our clique. But she didn't like clocks, so we were never early. Brian didn't really smoke pot, didn't like it so much; but he loved to drink. So pretty much I left smoking and took up drinking. I drank super heavy my senior year, super, super heavy, and tripping on acid too—but only three times after that.

After graduating from high school, I started hanging out again with Lisa. I guess it was a year or probably two years later—I was kinda tired of my high school boyfriend—and I started smoking more pot with my girlfriend and thinking there was a bigger world outside of Brian, you know what I mean? There were a lot of things he did that got on my nerves really bad. Then I's like, Hmm, nobody stays with a high school sweetheart forever, so I broke up with him and quit drinking. After that I just smoked pot with my girlfriend. And I've never quit since. I do love marijuana. I really wanted away from my parents, and I guess it was mainly because of Mom. Dad never got on my nerves that bad, it was always Mom that drove me nuts.

When I was twenty-one, I was in college, but I didn't have a major picked out. I was really stupid: to me it was like the world was gonna end in seven years. So, okay, I don't know why, but I just thought, You know, if the world wouldn't be around that much longer, why go to college? I couldn't go back for a semester anyway because I'd been put on probation for failing math so many times. I thought my parents were strict and I wanted to be grown up and I wanted to move out of my parents' house really bad and I had met a guy, Jason, that I dated for maybe six months—so I moved in with Jason. Then, sure enough, as Mama had warned me, "If you don't even know what your major is and if you're gonna live with this guy I don't even like, I'm not gonna pay any more tuition or anything." And now some twenty years later, she says, "I never said that, I never." But I can remember it clear as day. "Well," I said, "that's fine"—I was stupid and didn't realize how important education was at the time.

Jason, the guy I moved in with, was the one I later married. I met him at a rough bar on the edge of town.

I had called Lisa, my best friend, and her dad answered the phone. He was like, you know, "She hasn't been home in two days. And if you know where she's at, tell her she needs to get home. She has a baby now, and me and her mom—we're the ones raising this baby. So if you see her, tell her to get her ass home." It made me mad that she was neglecting her baby, so I'm gonna find her. This was before cell phones. So I went to this bar because I knew that her and her husband met there a lot. Her husband came from a big, alcoholic, dysfunctional, abusive family too. But she thought she could make the situation better, so they got married right out of high school. Then, like bam! right after that she got pregnant. Then, bam! once she was pregnant, he started beating her. He turned out to be a huge jerk. It only took about two times for him to hit her that she's like, Forget you. And after he hit her once when she was pregnant, she never went back.

Anyway I went to the bar that night looking for her. She wasn't there, but I knew somebody else that was there, her husband. And he was like, "Stay and have a drink with me." So I was drinking a beer with him, and I was sorta talking to some other girl that was there when, the next thing, Jason came up and said, "You want to be my partner in pool?" That's how we met. Then in a little while he said, "Do you get high, you smoke pot?" I said, "Yeah," and he's like, "You want to drive around and smoke a joint?" And I said, "Yeah." And I did that, and for some reason I later took him a puppy. I knew someone who had puppies, and he said he wanted a puppy. So I took him the puppy.

I was twenty-one or twenty-two when I met Jason, and we were together for seven years before we got married. Then six months after we married, he got murdered in a drug deal gone bad. He was a big alcoholic, drank all the time, always had one in his hand. He was from Virginia outside Washington, DC. There were a lot of gangs and crack and other drugs up there. He'd been involved in drugs real heavy, and he'd gone to jail a bunch of times. He came from a real good family. His father was the chief electrical inspector for the county, so his father's friends and even the police would call to warn his parents: "There's a big arrest gonna go down again, and you need to get your son out of here now, or he's gonna get hemmed up in this—there's no around it, just get him out of town so he won't get arrested. We're gonna bust in on them, and more than likely your son's gonna be there. So if he gets locked up again—he's been in so much trouble—he'll be gone for a really long time."

Jason was four years older than me, so he'd be like twenty-four, twenty-five. His parents moved him down to his grandmother's, who lived in a little mountain area in East Tennessee. So he went from a house in Washington, DC, to a little mountain one—a lot of culture shock, you know. He was an electrician and later moved in with somebody he worked with. After Jason and I dated for a few months, we got a place of our own. It was upstairs in a building owned by his boss. We didn't have to pay rent as long as Jason worked on fixing the place up. It was such a shit-hole, and my mama was like, "What are you doing?

Have you lost your mind?" And she said, "I won't give you so much as a blanket. Don't even ask me for a blanket." And I said, "I won't." And of course I did, and I have.

Jason would always smoke pot around me, and he drank. Years later Lisa started selling Xanaxes from a really good Xanax connection, and she was getting hundreds and hundreds of Xanaxes—no Valiums, "blue rounds." Then we got addicted to those and started taking them pretty hard. But Jason would get on crack binges, because that was his drug of choice. It was like cocaine, but I guess he couldn't find cocaine and he'd just do crack. He'd be good for six months and then be off and gone for days—and spend all his money. He made good money, but he spent it all on crack. He lied to me about what he was doing because I hated crack. So I never knew until he didn't come home at night or wouldn't come home for two or three nights. But like he'd be out smoking crack. He even traded my car one time for some crack. Told me he was going to the junk store and he'd be right back. He didn't come back, you know, and I didn't know where to find him. Me and his mom were close, but I didn't tell her half the time because I didn't want to upset her. She'd get real upset because he had such a bad life up near Washington with drugs and the law.

But I found my car. I went down to the car wash in the black part of town, because I was afraid he had backslid. And I found a little black dude driving my car. I thought, What the hell? And he was like, "Somebody sold me this car." And well, I was like, "They couldn't sell it to you because it's mine, and nobody has the title but me." I didn't say much more because I was young and timid and scared—they were black drug dealers. I really wasn't scared so much of just him, so me and my friend Sue, that was with me, followed him to his house. He told me if I gave him 250 dollars, I could have my car back. He kept saying, "I don't even want to talk with you because you're gonna call the law." I said, "I swear I won't. I just want my car back, just want my car back." If I had it to do all over again, I'd be like, "Give me my damn car and get the hell out, or I'll call 911." But I was so scared that they were gonna beat Jason up when they saw him again, you know, that I just wanted to do whatever they wanted me to do to get my car back. So I gave them 250 dollars, and my boss took me down there to get my car. But I did press charges against the black guy for "loss after a trust" because when you give someone that you trust, let somebody borrow your car, and they do something like he did, you can charge them—and I did have him arrested for that.

Jason and my daddy were real close. My daddy absolutely loved him. And he was borrowing money off my father left and right, I guess for crack. I didn't know about it because he worked and had a good job, making good money. The day he died, he borrowed like two hundred dollars from my daddy. And Jason told me he was going to Auto Zone. He had like a hot-rod Nova that he absolutely loved. He told me he'd be right back. But he didn't come back. And that would happen a lot when he was on his crack binges—and in seven years there were a lot of crack binges. I'd call the jails and the hospitals, give them his name, and say, "Do you have him?" Only that time when I called the police and asked, they said, "Hold on a minute." And the next voice came on said, "Criminal Investigation Unit." And I asked if they had him in custody, and they said, "Who is this?" I's like, "His wife." And they said, "Where you at?" (I had gone to my sister's to babysit since we were pretty close at that time and her kids were little.) I told them, and they said they'd be there in a minute.

My friend Sue was babysitting with me. She had grown up right beside me, and was like part of my family. She had a real shitty mom, and since her mom wouldn't come home at night when Sue was little, my family kind of like adopted her. Anyway I told Sue, "I'm getting ready to get arrested"— I thought I'm about to get arrested for selling pot. And I told her, "Take the kids to the front of the house—I don't want them to see nothing." I said, "I don't know what to tell my sister. Will you stay here with the kids?" And she said, "Yeah." And I said, "Just call Mom and Dad." So the police came up to the door, and one just said right away, "Are you Carol?" I say, "Yeah." And he said, "Jason's dead. We need you to get in the car." And I's like, "What?" He was a real asshole. There was one asshole cop and one nice cop. They told me that it was a young black boy who killed Jason, a boy that tried to sell him fake crack. (In court, the black boy said he "ganked" him, and that means he sold him fake crack on purpose.) There were actually two black guys that got in Jason's car to sell him the crack, and the three of them drove around the block. When the smaller one sold my husband the stuff, Jason looked at it like, "This ain't crack." The boy had Jason's money and, at that point, tried to get out of the car. But my husband grabbed hold of him, and the boy shot him—seventeen years old. The two guys jumped out and got in a car with two other black guys.

The four black guys drove back to a bar that used to be down beside the car wash. It was a bar they all went to, and they said that the youngest one went into the bathroom and threw up. He got down on his knees and started praying. That's how the four of them finally got busted. The detectives were going around, saying, "Seen anything, seen anything, seen anything?" Someone's like, "Well, I know Little Bobby was saved. We saw him on his knees praying, crying that night down at the bar, saying, 'Lord, please forgive me.' Maybe that could be it." And come to find out, that's what it was. Little Bobby was the youngest of the four black guys. He was probably only fifteen or sixteen. The first time we went to trial, he didn't show up to court; and we could hear a group out in the hall arguing—the killer's family were saying to the others, "You just tell your nephew that he needs to keep his mouth shut. He didn't do nothin'. He needs to keep his mouth shut." And that's why the little boy didn't show up to court the first time, because he was so scared of the killer's family. It seemed he wanted to tell the truth, but like, If I tell the truth, I still have to live in the same neighborhood with these people.

Anyway, the seventeen-year-old boy, that killed Jason, got off with only a year and a half because he got appointed a very good lawyer. My husband had the state district attorney to plead his case. I kept thinking, Is this really happening? Is this really happening? When the verdict came out, they found him guilty of reckless homicide. But he was going up for second-degree murder during a felony. He had a gun and robbed in the process. If you're committing a felony and you kill somebody while you're committing that felony, it's supposed to be an automatic big-time sentence, something heavier than reckless homicide. And the judge looked at the jury and said, "You twelve just let a guilty man walk free."

After that I stayed angry a long, long time—angry, angry.

And I really fell apart. I'd go to work drunk and just stay drunk pretty much all the time. The produce market where I worked was run by the man and his wife that owned it. Me and him were real close, real good friends. And I'd bring a cooler full of beer and put it in my sippy glass. He'd just let me drink it. One day I went to a bar for lunch, and I called him like, "I'm really drunk and can't drive back." And he's like, "Well, you need to get back. I'll send a taxi for you." I was like, "William, I'm really drunk. You don't want me touching your money and waiting on customers while I'm slurring my speech or falling around." He's like, "It's only two or three hours left, Carol, so come on now." He sent a taxi after me. I needed the job, and he was good to keep me on like that. But since I didn't make that much at the market and Jason had been the main breadwinner, I had to move in with Mom and Dad. But that didn't last very long at all, and in July I got a cabin off the highway a little out of town.

Jason died in January, and I met Scott in December of

that year. Scott was visiting his mother, a neighbor of mine, for Christmas and never went back. His mother was a real hoot. She was big, heavyset, and sarcastic—she was like a biker bitch. She liked Harley-Davidsons, and she was hard core. But she was a good person, she had a heart of gold. Scott and I started dating probably in February. So he was with me during the murder trial and stuff, but he didn't go to court with me or anything like that. I just didn't want to tell Jason's parents that I was dating somebody.

I kept up the drinking and always the pot, but no other drugs until the doctor prescribed me Xanax. I got addicted to those. I took a lot of downers. I would take the purple ones, which was 10 mg or whatever, you know—like six a day and drinking. I was a big mess when Scott met me. I really was. I think I quit taking those Xanaxes so much when I went to the murder trial because they had me on Xanax and Paxil. And the Paxil had just totally deadened my emotions: I didn't get happy, didn't get sad, didn't get mad. I had this rage, this low, deep rage inside me; but as far as really having an outburst, get mad or something— just didn't do that. I's just numb, didn't feel nothing. And I didn't want to go into my husband's murder trial and sit there emotionless. I kinda felt like, You bitch about street drugs; but, damn, you're just numbing me with this Paxil. It's the same thing that other drugs are doing, just deadening your emotions. I'd rather feel something at the trial than feel nothing at all; so the doctor said like, "Just try to do without the Xanax too." And I guess that's when I stopped doing pills, right after Jason's murder trial and right after the boy who shot him got sentenced and everything. It was shortly after the trial and sentencing that I found out that I was pregnant; so I had to give up pills anyway.

I was really shocked when I found out that I was pregnant. I was thirty-two, never been pregnant before; and Scott's family was like a circus freak show, not a family I wanted to get married into. But I got married pretty soon after I got pregnant.

Scott was doing meth at the time. I kinda knew about it; but I'd never done it, and I didn't want to do it. Jason had just got murdered over crack, and I knew the problems it caused in his life. Speed, that type of speed—I didn't want anything to do with crystal meth. But Scott was getting meth from "Uncle" Richard, a truck driver who lived in one of the cabins near us and who dealt in crystal meth. Scott would go up there all the time, but he wouldn't take me because he knew I didn't like meth.

Soon we had to get out of the cabin, because the cabin was just a small living space with a ladder step going upstairs to a loft. And it was really unsafe. There's no way you could've raised a baby in just basically that one room. So we had to get out of there and get a bigger place. And once we had our daughter, Megan, and got away from Uncle Richard, Scott didn't do crystal meth so much. And he was a great man there in the beginning. Scott was a great father, a good dad. He wanted to do the right thing, be a dad, and stay away from the meth. And so he did. He'd only treat himself every now and then if he got a big paycheck or something. And for years he would do a little coke every paycheck, which he would cook into crack. I was always just a pothead. But Scott was in control. He has the ability to just spend thirty bucks on Friday night, and that's it. He didn't do it all weekend long, just do a little bit on Friday night. That was crack. You can get a gram of cocaine, and you can cook it up and turn it into crack—turn that gram of cocaine into like fifteen rocks of crack and sell the crack. That's why people do it, because you can make so much money, you know what I mean? Buy a little cocaine for nothing and rock it up. I never really much liked crack, but I like drugs and a buzz, so if somebody says, "You want a hit?" "Well, honey, yeah." But it always made me throw up every time we did it. So he was doing cocaine, crack, and a little meth only occasionally, because meth was hard to find there for a while. Seems like Uncle Richard always had it, but I don't know what happened to him about that time. They were still friends, and he was one of Scott's mother's best friends. And I don't know why they called him "Uncle" Richard, but he was a huge meth dealer. At one point we would loan Richard our car, and he would drive it to Atlanta and get a bunch of dope, come back, and give us a lot of dope just for letting him borrow our car. And that was it. It was a gravy train we knew wouldn't last forever, because things like this just don't last forever. And of course, it didn't.

I gave up the downers and just smoked pot until Megan was maybe three or four and my friend Lisa got a killer hookup on Lortabs. Then I got kind of addicted to pain-killers: Lortabs, Percocet, and things like that for a couple of years. I always liked them, but they weren't really available—you know, like buying aspirin—at that point, without her connection. But Lisa got to thinking, I don't want to do this, don't want to do this—Scott is gonna get mad. And Scott did get mad, because I would tell Lisa, "Give me some, and I'll pay you back when Scott gets paid." I had quit working when Megan was born, and I'd just stayed with her all the time and got addicted to the pills. So I'd owe Lisa 125 dollars for the pills I got all week. And I'd have to tell Scott what I owed when he got paid. He hated pills, and that really pissed him off. I could see why it'd make him mad—I get that. But I was addicted to Lortabs for a couple of years there, after Megan was born. I've never been able to take a downer like a Valium or a Xanax since I gave them up when I was pregnant—they just really knock me out. I don't know for the life of me how I ever took six, that many pills a day. I just couldn't do that now for nothing, I couldn't. It'd really knock me out.

A little later on we did hear some news of Uncle Richard. A guy came over to tell us that a friend of Uncle Richard's who was living with him got pulled over by the cops. And that friend had a whole lot of money and a whole lot of drugs with him. And the cops took him to jail. The friend called Richard from jail and told him, "I'm in jail, and they say they're coming out to our house because they're suspicious about it." So Richard takes all the dope and is flying out of the house before the cops get there when he passes the cops on the way. He's going like ninety, and he threw all his dope out the window. But he got arrested anyway and went to federal prison. During his trial we didn't go because we were keeping our distance. We weren't gonna visit, call, or nothing. His son would come by and tell us what went on each day in court, you know. Well, he told us Uncle Richard had kept calling his girlfriend from jail. And he called us too the first night to tell us to go get the dope that he'd thrown out the window. But when an inmate calls, you're supposed to hit number one to accept the collect call and number two to decline, you know. And I really did mean to accept his call, but by accident I hit number two, to decline. And I was so grateful I did, because Scott would have gone to the field to get the dope and got caught. He would have. And since we didn't answer, Richard called his girlfriend and told her, "Go to that field where I threw my dope out. And the only people I want you to sell it to is Robert and Scott." Of course he was calling on a jailhouse phone, and the call was being recorded. She didn't know and went and got his dope. Then when it all went to court, his son told us that they were playing the recorded call and stopped the tape to ask, "Who is Robert and Scott?"

But we were scared to death anyway because after Richard's girlfriend got Richard's message and then the drugs, she immediately called Scott. And Scott had went up to the house and got a bunch of Richard's dope. I was in bed because I was pregnant with Tracy, and Scott was driving this car—I think it was stolen probably because he used to steal cars, not nothing around here, but he did. And we had a lot of cars you didn't have to have a key to start, you know, just turn the ignition if the key's not there. Well that was like our car at this time; you didn't have to have

a key to start it. But Scott forgot his keys when he was at
Richard's house, and then he realizes it when he was halfway home, at least ten miles away from Richard's. So Scott
is phoning up Richard's like three in the morning to say,
"Hey, I left my keys there. Hey, I left my keys there." And
the whole time the Feds are searching Richard's house! And
Scott had just left, I mean had just left. I'm sure the Feds are
like, "Why is Scott Fuller blowing your phone up at three
in the morning? Why?" And Scott is texting, "Hey, I just
left my keys there . . . I just left there . . . I left my keys . . .
put them up." So we were scared, petrified the whole time.
Plus I'm pregnant with Tracy and petrified that Scott was
gonna get in trouble and do time.

Richard's girlfriend did do federal time for her part selling the drugs. And it was a lot of dope. At the time it was
the most crystal meth they'd ever seen. And when Richard
got sentenced and put away, we thought, This is all behind
us, everything is great. Then a friend showed up, an old
friend showed up with some meth, and asked Scott to buy
some. And I threw a fit. I's like, "No, no, no." And Scott,
"Let's just treat ourselves, just treat ourselves this one time."
And I remember the friend was like, "I don't want to cause
any problems at all." He's like, "I wouldn't ever came if I'd
known it was gonna cause any trouble. I like both of you;
but, Scott, you should really listen to Carol. And I feel bad
and embarrassed that I'm even here doing this—and we're
leaving." Scott is like, "Don't pay no attention to her, at least
get *me* high, gotta get me high." And I, "If you say that you're
gonna get high—I didn't want to buy none . . . but— yeah,
I want to get high too." So we get high, and then it's like,

"Well, maybe you should buy a little." So meth came back into the picture. I like it all right. I wouldn't ever go out and spend my money on it, I really wouldn't; but if somebody like, "You want to hit this?" "Yeah." But I'm not gonna spend my money on it.

The next thing you know, after we started partying with this guy, somebody comes up to Scott with a buddy that knows how to cook crack. And if you spend a hundred dollars, they'll give you three times that just for letting them use your building. And Scott was like, "Okay." And they cooked crack in a little building in my backyard.

Scott already knew how to cook meth because he'd cooked it in Memphis. So after a while Scott started cooking meth in that building in the backyard. You have to have Sudafed to cook it and you've got to show your ID to get Sudafed and you can buy only so much. So that was always a problem getting Sudafed. But Scott cooked meth for over a year, and we were lucky to get away with it as long as we did. Little by little, everybody we were affiliated with started getting busted—somebody buying it or somebody telling on them or getting pulled over at a traffic stop. The law's not stupid, you know what I mean?

One night Scott goes up to Kroger's, because we lived like right behind Kroger's for about ten years. And the neighbors didn't like us because they found out we were cooking meth in our backyard. So he goes to Kroger's to like buy coffee filters—you need coffee filters in the meth-making process—and it was like three o'clock in the morning. He parked in the fire lane, exactly where I had got arrested a couple of weeks before that. And the night I was arrested, I was really high. We needed some cough medicine, so Scott handed me a hundred-dollar bill to go to Kroger's to get the medicine. And there I go into Kroger's intending to steal it because I's high and crazy—and, no question, I get caught. Scott was crazy mad at me. And I knew when I went in that I was gonna steal the cough medicine, so I took everything out of my purse except for my ID. I think that's all I had in there, or maybe a lipstick. It was like on a Sunday, and I said when they asked for my driver's license, "My other purse, I carried it to church today, and I hadn't transferred everything back into it." It was just an ID, not a driver's license, because I didn't have one. But the security guard knew it was my car in the fire lane. So when Scott went to Kroger's and the security guard saw Scott at three in the morning in the fire lane, he thought it was me. And the security guard's like, I'm gonna call those cops that are right up there at the restaurant and tell them to come pull her over for driving on a "suspended," because I know she don't have a license. And so he calls the cops, and instead of it being me, it's Scott. He didn't have a license either, and he has a car full of meth-making stuff.

So the cops come and sit in front of my house for like a half hour. And they're just sitting there. I'm thinking, What the hell are they doing? What the hell are they doing? I was freaking out because, I'm gonna get busted, I'm gonna get busted. I still thought, They're here to arrest me for meth. And then when I got to the door, and they're like, "We just pulled your husband over." And I'm just like, "Yeah, I know."

And so I bailed Scott out of jail, because they took him

to jail for driving on suspended. And when I picked him up, I's like, "Scott, they know something." I was like, "You know they sat out in front forever. They were like staking out, looking." I's like, "We don't have anybody that's left out here, you know what I mean? Everybody's in federal prison right now. You really think they're not onto us?" And he'd say, "I know, I know. I think they are." I said, "Look, I told you if you get my kids taken away from me, I swear, I'll kill you. I swear to God, I'll kill you." And he'd always say, "You don't know nothing about it. You tell them that we're down there in that building and that we go down there and play poker. Stay up here with the girls, and you ain't never gonna get in no trouble." And I'd say, "Yeah, I am. I'm your wife, and whatever charges you get, they're gonna give me." He'd say, "No, you won't—no you won't." Well, yeah, I did . . . but when it was all said and done with, I really didn't.

The cops did come back the following week. And I was getting ready to lay the girls down for bed; and then bang, bang, bang, real loud on the door. Scott wasn't there. I figured it was gonna be one of our friends or next-door neighbor that was coming around all the time. I definitely didn't think it was gonna be the cops. My heart went, Oh, my God, that's what I feared for the past some twenty years. The cops do scare me because Jason dealt in a little bit of weed and stuff. I said, "You need to talk with Scott, and he's not here." But they said right off, "We know what's going on here, We pretty well know. We just need you to fill in some blanks for us." And I's like, "I don't know what you're talking about: 'what's going on here?' I need to get my girls in bed, though, and get them asleep. You're kinda freaking them out." One cop was like, "Do you realize I could take your kids from you right now?"

Well, when that cop said, "You realize we could take your kids from you," I said, "For my house being so dirty?" And he said, "Ma'am, quit acting stupid, quit playing stupid." I said, "I'm not playing, I really don't know why you'd take my kids away from me. I realize the house is dirty, but I don't think it's that dirty."

I was worried about how the house looked because Scott was always on me about keeping the house clean. "Don't let the house get dirty because that's what meth heads do. We don't want to have someone come in here and see us living like trash, because that'll be a number-one sign, a tipoff." Well, our washing machine and our dishwasher went out at the same time. And there was a shitload of clothes when you first walk in that I's getting ready to do. And of course the dishes—I don't like handwashing dishes, I really don't. I's like, I'll just wait until we buy another dishwasher, and just use paper now. That was my plan.

Just then I saw Scott come walking down our dead-end street, and I said, "That's who you need to talk with, right there." And I shut the door. The next thing you know, Scott opens the door with all of the cops and starts talking. And I'm here like, Why are you telling them all that stuff? You're telling things they aren't even asking. But then they had told Scott, "Just tell us everything, we'll leave your wife here tonight." And they told me that the girls could too, but I didn't believe them and said, "I don't believe you motherfuckers.

You're gonna call the Department of Children Services. I'm getting my kids out of here *now*." So I called a friend to come and get my girls right then—and got them out of there. But the DCS went and got my girls the next day.

Anyway, the cops took us to jail, both Scott and me, that night. They said, "Mrs. Fuller, you might want to light that cigarette up." And I said, "Why?" And he said, "Well, you're getting ready for a long ride to the county jail." And I got up and started hitting Scott. And I'm really mad at him, "You got me hemmed up in this. I mean I'm gonna kill ya." And the cop said, "Don't be mean to him; you got warrants on you anyway." And I said, "What for?" And he said, "For buying Sudafeds." And I said, "I never went over my limit." He said, "Well, you can't buy them to make meth, dumbass." It's funny now, nine years later—that night it wasn't funny at all.

When I went to jail, the first night I went there, a woman read off all these charges. And I'm like, "I'm not guilty of none of them. The only thing I'm guilty of—and I'm not even being charged with—is that I was buying boxes of Sudafeds. I am guilty of buying boxes, and that ain't even one of my damn charges."

And being in jail traumatized me. I don't know how people do it. They come in and go out all the time like it is nothing; but I was thinking, I'll never see my girls again. Scott had a lab, and we had a lot of "stuff." I was like, I'm gonna get twenty years. I'm never going to see Megan and Tracy get married or graduate or anything. So I cried for like three months.

Scott did say—he used to be a good man, I mean that serious—he would always say, "I will take all the rap, I will take all the rap if we get in trouble." And we got in trouble, and Scott did take all the rap. He said, "She never wanted to buy boxes of Sudafed; if she didn't buy them, I wouldn't give her the car or I wouldn't buy her cigarettes or sometimes I'd hit her." And that was never true. I mean, I bought that Sudafed willingly because I wanted to get high, I did. But other than buying Sudafed, I don't know the first thing about how to cook meth. But I got all of Scott's charges too.

Every time I'd go to court—which you go like every month—the DA would stand up and say, "The State's not gonna indict them because the Feds are." And one time I raised my hand, because I had a public defender; and I said, "What does *indict* mean?" And the judge said, "It means if we have enough evidence to charge you with crimes you're being charged with." And I said, "I've sat in here for six months, and you don't know if you have enough evidence to charge me with?" And he said, "She's right. You got somewhere to go today?" And I was like, "Yeah, my mama's." And Mama's like, "You really want to go there?" And he said, "Can she come to your house?" And Mama said, "Yeah." So they let me out. And I was under house arrest after that, waiting to be sentenced.

And I went to court one time, and the judge was like, "I have a warrant for your arrest for seventy-four counts of promotion of methamphetamine." And he's like, "Bailiff, take her next door," to the jail. And, thank God, my house-arrest officer was there that day; and he stood up for me and said, "Please don't take her to jail." And the judge said to me, "You have him to thank."

And one woman who was a state worker said, "Your children are now the custody of the state." That was worse than Jason's death in the car. That was just awful. So my children lived with my sister, and I lived with my mom. The visitations were supposed to be supervised by Mom being present, and my sister was to go by the rules. And she would never be lenient at all with me and let me see my children at her house. I'm like, "Really, Angela, really? They're *my* children." But my sister is a bitch, she's a bitch. But she was so mad at me for everything, she was not going to break any rules.

I didn't have the kids, but I'd do certain things where I could get them back again. I had three jobs at one point— they were all part-time jobs, but I had three of them. I paid all my fines, I passed all the drug tests, and the judge was like, "His wife's doing this good, we should let him out too." Scott had served eleven months down at the county jail, and the judge was in a good mood one day and said, "I'm let you sign your own bond and put you on house arrest, because your wife is out." So they let Scott out on house arrest until he got sentenced.

Finally, the Feds decided that they weren't going to indict us and that the State could go ahead and indict us. When the State did, we went to sign our plea on initiation to process meth—I don't really know what that means, I guess it means to mix it all together and cook it. That carries twelve years in prison, and like we'd been going through court for a year and a half. We got busted in April of 2009, and it wasn't finalized until November of 2010. And Scott was like, "I'm ready to get this over with. I'm tired of going to court every month and sweating this. I'm just going to sign it and pray for the best." And I's like, "Well, I'm pissed off. Damn, that's twelve years."

While we were in the public defender's office, I got this woman lawyer—not the guy that I did have who wouldn't ever say nothing. He wouldn't tell me a damn thing any time we'd get called up. I thought, What good are you? You didn't say, "Hi," "bye," or wave—I mean nothing. But this public defender said, "Will you go step outside because cell phones don't get signal back here in this office." And I said, "That's fine because I want to smoke a cigarette anyway." So I went outside, and I lit a cigarette up. She said, "I can tell you are upset." And I said, "Yeah, I'm real pissed off." She said, "You want to talk away from your husband?" I said, "No, I'll talk in front of him. He knows I'm pissed off. I told him that he's cooking meth and he's getting my kids taken away from me and I'm going to prison for all that." And I said, "I swear, I never cooked meth. I haven't. I've smoked a shitload of it, and I did buy boxes of allergy pills. I did." I said, "But past buying them boxes, I ain't done none of these things you're charging me with." And she's like, "Whatever, you need to go back in and sign that plea." At this point I was pleading out to everything they were charging me with, like seventy-four counts of boxes, maintaining a dwelling where boxes are sold, and aggravated child abuse and neglect. And one of the lawyers there said to me, "I'll tell you right now"—

because they also appointed the girls lawyers to talk on their behalf—"I'll tell you right now, there's a fifty-fifty chance you'll never get the custody of your children back again." So I looked at my lawyer and said, "Is that true?" And she said, "Kinda. You can get them back, but you're just gonna have to work really hard."

So I signed the plea, and went to court two days later. And she looked at me, and she said, "I thought about you so much that, when you left the other day, I took yesterday off so I could sit at home in my pajamas and smoke my cigarettes and drink my coffee and read through your files." She said, "Really, they don't have anything on you past buying boxes. They can't prove you've done nothing else." And she said, "I called the DA at home at midnight and told him, 'I'm not gonna let Carol plead out to all these charges because you can't charge her with something you don't have any evidence for.' And he said, 'Well, that's fine. I don't want her anyhow. I just want her husband.'" So I plead to two boxes, buying just two boxes, which really I had bought lots—three a month for years. They call it promotion, promotion of methamphetamine—that's when you buy a box of Sudafed, called promotion. And Scott took all the rap. I got two years' unsupervised probation, and I didn't have to report or anything. Scott got eight years' probation, which meant he had to report every month, give them fifty dollars, and have a drug test. We went home that day. So I got out of jail in October, first of October 2010. And the kids could finally come live with me and Scott in May. We got a place, and then we got final custody in August.

Then in January 2012 US Marshals come knocking on
our door and took Scott to federal prison. They charged
him with conspiracy, because he came out of the county
jail and started buying boxes again. I didn't know it. He
was buying Sudafed again and cooking meth. There were
a few hints that made me think, you know; but I'm like,
There's no way in hell, no way in hell, would he be doing
that again. He wouldn't put me and the girls through that
again. But I'd find things he'd used to make meth with, like
a little fishing tube. And I said, "Why did you buy fishing
tube?" He's like, "Why, I'm gonna put it, you know, in a fish
tank." Then lithium batteries. Then I found Sudafed one
night. I's like, "Please tell me you're not . . . because we're
on the list . . . we can't even buy it." His lawyer told him,
"They really want you, the Feds really want you. Whatever
you do, you know, you better behave; and, surely, don't buy
no boxes." He said, "Well, I won't buy no boxes." And he
came right out and started buying boxes again. That's why
the Feds came back and got him. He was passing his drug
tests because meth doesn't, like, stay in your system but for
two days. So once he had his appointment each month, he
knew he was good for another month. He'd stop a couple of
days before his appointment, and he was good to go. Meth
is one of the most evilest drugs, but it stays in your system
the least amount of time of anything else.

After I got out of jail on house arrest and before I got
the kids back and was living with my mother, I didn't have
a driver's license and I had to bum rides with everybody to
get to work. But my sister's friend owned a company in a

building that had an apartment upstairs. And she said, "If it'll help you to get your girls back faster, you could live up there. No charge for rent or water, just pay the electric and cable if you want cable." That was one block from a bad part of town; and since Scott was still in jail, I'm kinda scared to live there by myself. But me and her went to look at it. It'd been like ten years empty, and it was so nasty. It just looked horrible. I was miserable down at Mom's, and the apartment was walking distance to town; but I thought, I can't do this. Then Scott got out of jail, and he said to my sister's friend, "I can fix it up for you if you're willing to pay for the materials and stuff." Scott is real good at remodeling. We painted it, hauled all the carpet out, and put down stuff that looks like hardwood floor. But we didn't have a yard, and I always thought that was one thing caused Scott to become bored and start cooking meth again. Scott really likes a yard and flowers and being outside. But at that second-floor apartment we had a parking lot, and that was it. It drove him crazy and it drove me crazy. I couldn't stand it there, I hated it there. I really hated it.

One day my sister's friend called me, and she's like, "I hate even to tell you this, because I know you're in a spot"— I wasn't working, and Scott at the time has been taken back to prison—"but we're selling the place, and you and the kids need to find yourself somewhere else to live." She said, "Don't give me any more rent money." At this point after we got it fixed up, it was nice. I was like, "We can't just live here and not be giving you no rent money. It's not trashy up there anymore, it looks nice. So let me give you something."

She's like, "I don't know . . . a hundred dollars." "No, more than a hundred dollars, because you can't rent no place for a hundred dollars. That's taking advantage of you." And she said, "One twenty-five." I'm like, "I'm gonna give you at least two hundred. Even that is crazy cheap. You can't rent no place for two hundred dollars." We should have moved out before then, but we got accustomed to being there because the bills were so low and we were having a ton of extra money. But then they sold the place, and there I was left screwed.

And I asked this man I know who had some properties if he had anyplace to rent. And he said he would help me out until I got on my feet. That's *all* I done, was to ask. And I moved into a place in June 2012. He lied and didn't help. Then Scott got out of prison in June of 2015. But he had to stay in a halfway house in Knoxville until Christmas Eve. He was home from Christmas Eve till the end of August. Then he took up with a young woman who was a druggie. And she was convicted in the three surrounding counties—she was on a three-county tour!

This is why Karma is a bitch. On December 16th, Scott stopped by his probation officer's to ask some question, like could he postpone an appointment, or something like that. She said, "Yeah, but first, I want you to take a drug test." And he failed it. His stupid girlfriend sat out in the car like for four hours before she went in and said, "My boyfriend came in here a long time ago, and he didn't come out." "Well, he's down there at the county jail." And he was there from December until July when they sentenced him and sent him off to federal prison in Kentucky. And he's still there.

The only reason I know what happened is that Scott's girlfriend tried buddying up with Scott's brother, and he told me all about it. He's been my brother-in-law for eighteen years, and we've always been pretty tight. I don't even know how much time Scott got because me and Scott don't talk. Now Scott lies to his brother because he knows that his brother is telling me what he says. He did tell my sister on a phone call, before he got taken away to federal prison, that he writes the children all the time and I'm not giving them the letters. And he's really not doing that. I wish he was. I really wish he would write his girls. But he's only wrote them one time. Scott doesn't want me to know anything, but Scott's girlfriend has called his brother a couple of times, asking for money to put on Scott's account in prison to buy supplies and snacks. She has known Scott's family forever since her mother was best friends with Scott's mother. And I even knew that the girlfriend had a crush on Scott when me and Scott first met, when she was like thirteen or fourteen. She made it really obvious, but Scott was like twenty-six at the time, and I didn't think nothing about it. Nobody did, you know. But now that she's thirty-two, Scott and her say they're gonna get married and everything. I don't know. You think you know somebody after twenty years, you know what I mean?

I'm surviving financially, but I'm still behind in my rent. My landlord's compassionate, but they're to the point now like, We're tired of being compassionate. And this guy Bob, that's staying in my house now, is the only one I've let come in. And the only reason I let him is that he helps with the bills. I didn't even let him in for some time; but after awhile, I couldn't get him out. He wouldn't leave. I thought, Well, he'll help foot the bills, you know. But he's been there for six months, and he's only given me three hundred dollars. And it's like, "Bob, my electric is at least two, two-twenty, two-fifty sometimes." It's just like, he don't realize how much it costs me to live. I sell plasma, I work a part-time job, I have a little side hustle, and, you know, beg Peter to pay Paul. And that's the way I've been living because Scott is locked up and can't give me child support. And I can't get any kind of State help, Social Security, or a lot of financial help—like a lot of other people get—because I've got those drug charges.

And I can't get food stamps, but the girls can since they're just seventeen and twelve. And for food stamps they make you go up for renewal like every six months. I would tell them the truth, like I always do, and they would always mess up and send me a letter, saying, "You are *approved* for food stamps, and here's how much you get." Then like two months later, they catch on that I wasn't supposed to get them, and they'd send me a letter, saying, "We're cutting yours, but your daughters still get theirs." That went on for a couple of years. I never lied to them the whole time. I'd tell them the truth, and they'd mail me a letter that would say, "You are approved." So it's not like I was skinning them, but I did know better. Well then, one time instead of saying, "We're gonna take those away"—it's now, "You owe us all that money we gave you for food stamps. You owe us that back." And I's like, "No, I don't! No, I don't! I didn't lie to you, I told you the truth. And you told me that I was approved, and that's why I spent that money. I got a letter that I was approved and it was all right." And they were like, "I know, it is no way fair. It says right here that it's your case worker's flub and mess-up day; but they are going to make you pay it back, honey." I said, "Well, I work at a grocery store, and every girl I was in jail with comes through with food-stamps cards. Why can't I?" "Well, certain drugs, they're harder on. You got meth charges." "Yeah, I know." "So you can either pay us this money back one month at a time, or we're gonna take a little bit of your children's food stamps till it's paid back up." I's like, "Well, take some of the food stamps till it's paid back up, because I don't have 399 dollars to give you."

I am barely surviving, but I don't want to do drugs or get into drugs anymore. I do a little weed, but I don't think weed is really a drug. I think it's gonna be legal. I do like pot. Thank God, I've lived here long enough in my life that I have a lot of friends—like the little Beatles song, "I get high with a little help from my friends." I got enough friends that'll give you a little pinch of bud, and I can afford a little bit. Weed's kinda like my medicine. I get anxious, and it calms you down—it does. And I think it's better than a Valium or Xanax, you know. And so I always have a little bit of weed.

It's hard to maintain just being alive when it's harsh; but people can't do hard drugs every day, you can't. People who do them every day wonder why your life is falling apart. I mean, damn, you just can't do hard drugs every day and maintain a normal life or a normal relationship or anything—you can't. I learned my lesson. I told Scott when I found that little fish tube, "Did you not learn anything the first time?" And he said, "Yes—that I want to be kinda smarter than them." And I's like, "I always knew you were a little stupid, but I never knew how stupid you was till you said that. They don't come no smarter, Scott. They have equipment, like electronic equipment that they could listen to us right now. Damn, they just don't come no smarter than them, and I can't believe you said that." But *that* got him right back in federal prison, you know. Idiot! I don't hate him for leaving me—I can understand that and I can get over that—but I do hate him for the family that he took away, our family unit.

Good things will happen, they will. I'm like a cat. I land on my feet, I do. They made me see a shrink to get my girls back one time when I got in all that trouble. And the shrink said, "She has the ability to get knocked down and get right back up." Hard knocks don't really faze me too much, nothing does too much—unless it's with my kids. If it deals with them, if they're affected, that's the only thing that affects me too much. I grew up with a mom and dad. My dad was an asshole to Mom. And lots of times I wished she'd divorce him, because he talked to her like shit. One time I's in the backseat of the car, and I'd think, I'll never, ever let a man talk to me like that. He treated me like gold, he's real good to me. But he'd talk like shit to Mom. That's why me and this guy, Bob, fight so, because if you take a soft tone with me and just don't be an asshole to me, we'll be okay. And Bob's an asshole. So I don't know what I'm gonna do with him . . . kick him to the curb? I don't want to call the law, but I'm afraid that's what it's gonna come to.

Although I'm not selling any drugs, I wish I could get a good hookup on it. I did when Scott was in prison. I did have a good hookup on pot. I was getting it dirt cheap and just flip it and make a little bit. But when I wrecked my car—like right after that pretty much—I ran out of time on my phone. It's like I'm depressed: I don't care about time on my phone, I don't care about my customers, I don't care who's trying to get in touch with me, and I didn't do nothing for about two weeks. Then when I got out of it and try to call my little weed-dude, he'd already changed his number, and I can't find it again. And I didn't want to go to his house because he was mixed, like half black/half white, but his girlfriend was like this crazy little Puerto Rican. She just looked like a crazy bitch, and I didn't want to go up there and knock unannounced and everything. Plus he always had a bunch of friends over, you know, a bunch of black kids. I just didn't want to go knocking on the door there—I just feel uncomfortable—so I just let that connection go. But now, I wouldn't even be really able to get rid of it. The thought I have constantly is how can I turn fifty dollars into a hundred, and how can I turn this hundred into two hundred. My main job now is the part-time job, and I have two people every week or so that I clean their houses and do their laundry. And I have that little hustle which is, let's say, fifty a week. Somehow, I always make it. And I love TV—I'm addicted to it—but I don't have cable now. We had cable until Scott left; and my last two cable bills, when he was there, was like 350 dollars, because he watched so much porn. He'd watch it on the big-screen TV and have it in his hand on the phone. And I's like, "Damn, Scott!" I was really mad when our cable was two hundred, but 350 bucks—that's just crazy, that's just crazy. And so that last time, the month he left, I couldn't pay it. So I just let it slide.

I guess I've been pretty strong to get through all this, but I tell my girls all the time, "When things are bad, it won't always be like that. It's not always gonna be bad." But when times are good, they have to remember, "It's not always gonna be good, it's gonna get bad again. It's gonna be good, it's gonna get bad again"—that's just life, you know what I mean? A lot of this stuff for me has been the result of drugs, but I don't really regret any of it. It's been fun, you know. When I look back on the memories I have— you know, there's people that say they've been so bored or whatever. Well, damn, my life's not boring at all, you know what I mean? I can tell you some stories, I mean I've done some shit. So now I don't regret it because I wouldn't have all those crazy experiences. Sometimes I think about my sister, Ah, you're so boring, your life is so boring. Sometimes, you know, I'm a little jealous—it'd be nice to have a little of the material things she has, you know. But then I think, You don't have nowhere near the experiences that I've had. Those things that I think have been fun, she don't think they're so much fun—but we're cut from a different cloth.

From this point on I would like to have more money; and I would like to have some guy I cared about and could depend on, I would. But I don't think that's gonna happen until I do it for myself. I don't think there's gonna be anybody until I get out of this hole somehow on my own.

As far as the future or where I see myself in it—as Scott would say, "You're just like a damn youth that goes with no target. You're just *going*. You don't know where in hell you're going, you're just out there." And I am. I don't like to make plans because I might not want to do whatever *that* is tomorrow. If I make plans, something might come up, and then I might want to do *that*. I don't like planning, and God's always took care of me, always has—never went hungry, without, or homeless. So I don't really like to think about *me*. And when I do, sometimes it scares me; so I don't. I want the good life, and that's why I'm gonna have to go back to school. I'm never gonna have a good life if I don't, because the good life is not struggling, not freaking out in being evicted or in not coming up with the electric bill or when the ends won't hook up. And I didn't have to struggle with all that when I had Scott. Then when he was locked up, I did have to think about all those things. And there for four years, the first time he was in federal prison, I kept saying, "It's almost over, it's almost over, it's almost over." And then—poof.

A Good Heart

Portrait: a black woman, born in 1961 to an impoverished family, who grew up in a small city (ca.
31,000 population). Her formal education includes
a diploma from a high school (ca. 1,500 enrollment), a business college associate's degree, and
a university bachelor's degree. She is the mother
of two sons.

Notable Personae: mother, fathers, four siblings, childhood girlfriends, boyfriend/husband, two sons,
and influential female employer.

Themes (among others): religious background, personal religious faith and beliefs, family com-
posite, father figure, parental authority, mother-
daughter relationship, childhood responsibilities,
self-esteem, work ethic, school counseling, employment, welfare, disability, poverty, finances,
drugs and drug addiction, incarceration, marital
relationship, racism, discouragement, and personal fortitude.

I never felt like I was in poverty, which I know I was, but I just felt like I always had what I really needed to feel comfortable, like good clothing to go to school. Of course, there were times we didn't have those things, but I just never felt the stigma of being what they call being really impoverished. Of course we was, because we lived in the Project. The income lets you know you're impoverished. And even though people probably view projects as being very bad, the Project was my best place. I loved where I lived. I had my own room and we kept it clean. There was four bedrooms. The brothers shared a room, my mom had a room, and my sister and I each had a room. And I enjoyed my childhood. That was really my best time. I could say we needed more money or something like that; but God, He's blessed us even when there were hard times and we didn't have anything to eat. My mama did the best she could. She would borrow money, and people would come and help us. The Project was probably not like it is today. But then you could leave your front and screen doors open. There was of course some bad stuff too, like drugs coming in around the Project—and I've tried marijuana; but it didn't get ahold of me, it didn't bring me to a point where I was addicted or something.

I had a certain group of friends I hung with, and I just had a good time with my friends. Of course I did things I shouldn't have done, like smoking marijuana, drinking, being promiscuous—that kind of stuff—but I was just trying to have a good time, trying to enjoy my friends. At one point we called ourselves a gang. It was five of us girls growing up, like twelve and thirteen. And if someone messed with one of us, then of course there would be action; but

I was just really hoping that nothing would happen. But there is some things that did happen. We did have to beat up people—then we got beat up too. And we did call ourselves a gang, but really we wasn't. We didn't have guns and stuff like they do now. And our "gang" just lasted about three years—we did it like when we was in junior high up to sometime in my high school years.

We did go to a club down there in the Project, even before we were of age. We slipped in. You were supposed to be eighteen, and they were supposed to card you; but the owners knew our parents, and they let us come in. And I continued to go to the club when I got out of school and didn't live with my mom, when I could do what I needed to do . . . wanted to do. And there was another black-owned club near downtown that I'd go to where all the blacks at that time went. But I never got into trouble. I just felt like God had his hand on me—it's just the way I see it.

I'm the oldest of five children. I have one sister and three brothers. My mother raised us up in a single home, and we didn't have a father figure. Most of us in the Project didn't have a father in the home. Normally, when you grow up there, you don't have a father because if you lived in the Project, you had to have a low income to qualify; and generally if you had a two-family income, you wouldn't qualify. If anybody that lived in the Project did have a father figure, it was one slipping in and out—it wasn't one married to their mom. So since everybody that lived around me kind of had the same situation, it didn't bother me, in a way, until later on that I didn't have a father figure.

My mom done well, I believe, with what resources she

had. She was able to keep her jobs and provide for us and buy our clothing. She was pretty strict because she was a pastor, and she brought us to church every Sunday. Every time the doors was open, we were there. I went to a couple of elementary schools, then junior high and high school. We just did the normal things that kids do going to school. And my mom was kinda liberal about what we did after school. Of course she taught us to do our homework and stuff, but she didn't kind of *make* us do it. Basically it fell on us: if we did it, we did it; if we didn't, we didn't. I was just glad that I liked school, and I carried about a 4.0 through junior high. But then in high school I got around some people, and my grades started dropping. I still averaged a 3.5, so it still was good. I just think I was blessed with a gift of liking to read. I did have peer pressure too, of course, to take up my time. Our thing was—my set of friends and me—we would go to the Rec, the recreational center in the Project, sports. That's where we hung out, and that was our social activity after school. That kept me busy, either playing sports or just being with my friends.

As far as my family, I was born in 1961, and my four siblings were born about every two years after me. We had different fathers. Me and the older brother next to me, we had the same father. Then the middle brother, he had a different father. Then the other two had a different father. I only seen my father twice. I kinda remember the first time—maybe I was one or two, I don't know—but he had a baseball hat that was orange. I can remember that. Then when I was probably about thirteen, my mom and my pastor at that time dressed me up, but they didn't tell me what I was gonna do. They just told me that they was taking me to the mall. But when we got to the mall, my mother went one way; and the pastor, she was like, "I'm gonna take you to meet someone." And inside one of the stores, there was a man that I didn't know dressed in a "clergy suit." I can just barely remember his face, but I know he had on a clergy suit with a white collar, and I think it was a black suit. And my pastor said, "This is your father." Of course I was kinda shocked, and I didn't know how to respond. When he came up to me, he just offered me like five dollars; and just then— I remember clearly—I don't want that and I'm ready to go. So I never seen him anymore. I heard he did pass. I think my mom has a hard time with men. She never wants to talk to me about the father figure.

Now my brother who has the same father as me, not knowing who his father was did affect him. He was the main one that would always say, "Don't you want to know your father?" I don't know if I just pushed it into the back of my mind, but I would always say, "No, I don't care. Just don't worry about it." Still there was something in him, even till he was an adult, looking for his father. I don't know if that caused him to have issues with his drug habit or not. When we did ask our mom about our father, she would say, "I'm your father and your mother, you don't need to know. He didn't do nothing for you, he's not gonna do nothing for you." So what else can you do?

The only way I found out information about my father was through my mom's friends or different people her age.

One of her best friends—I don't know if my mom told the lady to tell me or not—but once, mom's friend said, "Did you see your father? He was here at the convention at the church." I said, "No, where was he?" She said, "Aw, I don't know." I know my father was married and had a family, but at that time I really didn't want to know. I think I probably started thinking about it, maybe now and then, since I was like fifty. And then I just thought about it because somebody told me that he had passed. And I knew, he and his family were in North Carolina, and he was supposed to be a preacher. So it kind of affected me because I know it takes two to tango. I have tried to Google his name to see what I could find out, but I haven't found out anything. I know who to call if I do really want to know, but I just leave it like it is. I wonder sometimes, if I would have acted in another way (when I was a teenager and met my father) that maybe there would have been some kind of relationship between us. But I don't know if that would have made a difference in my life. I just feel like, even though it didn't happen, I have my faith, I have my heavenly father.

The father of my second brother, I didn't know either. His father was single when my brother was conceived, but he did get married later. My understanding was that he asked my mom to go with him to Washington, but she didn't want to go. So he left. And my brother never seen him, at least alive. I also don't remember ever seeing him until he passed. We did go to his funeral. So at least my brother did get to see him there. But the man's parents was always involved in my brother's life. They would get him clothes and things—so there was a connection there.

Then my third brother and my sister has another father. He was a married man. And I don't know exactly how my sister and youngest brother felt or feel about the matter of their father. Since we were young, we didn't realize at the time that the situation was adultery. We just learned about that as we got bigger. To me, my sister and brother turned out all right because their father would take the whole family riding on Sunday afternoon. He would pick us up, and he treated us like we was his kids too. But he died. It ended up, I think, that their father loved them and probably loved my mom too, because he had it set up where they could get his Social Security. And that brought a big issue within the family, because when she started receiving that check, then we were living off those two kids. So we're kind of dysfunctional. That was that chapter. But in spite of all that, I grew up.

After I was born, my mom lived in several different houses. We even had to live with a friend of hers. They was "grounded"—they was in the church—and they took us in, just me and my mama at that time. And then she got a house, but the house was in poor condition, and I really didn't like it. We had rodents and things. I hated it. Later, our whole family lived there—all five siblings. We stayed there until she got a place in the Project. That's where she found the church. She had a hard time, and she done some things growing up—till she got herself rooted, I guess. She drunk—she wasn't an alcoholic, but she did drink some. That was her way of escape, I guess. But she got into the church, and then that's how we got grounded in the church.

Since I was the oldest and Mama had to work, I had

responsibilities. I was the one that had to watch the children—not that they didn't take care of me. I was the one that had to cook. I was the one who had to keep the house clean and try to get everyone else in line. I was the one that had to answer if something wasn't right. My siblings would probably say that I was rough on them. And I probably was because I didn't want to get a whipping. But we all delegated—we would delegate the chores amongst each other: "This week, you do this, this is your week to wash dishes, this is your week to do the bathroom." We would do it like that. And sometimes they didn't want to do their jobs, sometimes I didn't want to. Then when it got to the place where they didn't do their chores, I was like, Well, what's going on?—I can't make them do anything. So I just started cleaning up only my room and the bathroom. Then everything else could go. My mom, as she would tell anyone, wasn't a good housekeeper; but I think it made her want to do better that I kept my part straight. She would say to me, "You like things clean"—"Yeah, I don't like dirt." So it made her do a little better, but she was always wore out.

My mom was pretty strict, but instead of disciplining us with a belt—though she did do that sometimes and even use extension cords or say, "Go get your own switch"—most of her discipline was verbal abuse. And with me she would holler and scream and call me all these names. I still struggle with some of the things she said to me. And I've addressed that with her, but today she still does things like that. Even though I love her to death and I have flaws as well, it caused me to have low self-esteem.

I feel like my mom, through the men she met, was maybe devastated and very hurt. Then with that and all the other load that she was carrying—five kids, that's a lot— she had to lash out sometimes. And sometimes it would be us. Maybe verbally was the only way she knew how to deal with it, her way to release. But I didn't like it. And it made me say that when I had my children, I wouldn't do them that way, no matter what.

I know that deep down she loved us, and she was a good mom in spite of all the circumstances. She didn't give up. She worked very hard with two or three jobs and did provide for us. She would go to Kress's, I believe it was called, and buy us the best clothing. And she really did try to get us anything we asked for. She got us a swing set, she got us dogs. She would try her best, and if she couldn't, she couldn't. She was also a pastor, and even though the church didn't have many members, probably two or three, she kept it going and paid the bills. Of course, we had to help her with the church. We put the coal in the stove, we helped her clean, and stuff like that. I think when she started going to church and pastoring, she enjoyed it. It was her faith, and it gave her, I believe, a sense of value and purpose.

But just to be honest, I still have trust issues with my mother. I don't feel like I can tell her anything, and I don't tell her anything. I have tried that. I'm sorry to say this, but to be truthful, she puts down her kids. She's our mother, but she makes us feel like we can't do anything. My sister even told her, "You don't think your kids are capable of anything because you will not stand up for us." In front of people she do, but behind our back, she talks about us. She gets on the phone and tells personal things that she shouldn't say. I guess I'm very angry with her right now, but I have to move on.

From an early age I always wanted to work. I knew we needed money to help with things. So that's what I did. At the age of fourteen I had my first job, at the VA, a summer job cleaning—it's called environmental services. It was one of the programs they have for low-income people, and I worked there each summer. I paid for my sister's clothing, and my mom would get the boys' clothing. My part was also to help with some of the other things, like the electric bill and the water bill. So it made me kind of responsible. That was good. I also wanted to have money to buy the normal stuff kids want, like going to a movie, although at one time my mom wouldn't let us go to a movie because of her belief.

During my senior year in school, my mom worked at a local company, and she asked me did I want a job there. I did, and I got a job as a machine operator. So I worked full time while going to school full time. They let me out of school at two, and I went to work from like three to eleven. I loved that job. I liked making money so I could buy my things. I liked things, I wanted things, like clothes and all. The job made a lot of money that I wasn't used to. And I think my work background also helped to keep me steady. It helped to keep me out of trouble. But I got laid off. Then I worked at another plant where all I did was load and put knobs on heaters. But I got laid off there too.

When I got out of high school, I feel like the system failed me, because I had a 3.5 average, but no counselor talked to me about school or anything. So I moved out from home and went on working at my jobs. Then I ended up pregnant, unmarried, when I was twenty-two; and me and my boyfriend—that would later become my husband—had our first child. We had got together when we were in high school . . . well junior high. I moved back home with my mom and got on welfare. I did the welfare thing because most people I knew was on welfare. On welfare you had housing (no charge) and food stamps (no charge). When I worked, I had to pay for everything. So when I found out that you get everything free, I thought, This is good, I'll just do this. Then after a year, still on welfare, I moved out of my mom's again and in with my boyfriend.

I still did some work like cleaning for this lady that had multiple sclerosis. I met her through my boyfriend's mother, who cleaned house for her. She was needing some assistance like blowing the leaves or cleaning the baseboards—all this kind of stuff. So I did it. It was her that told me as we talked that I should go to school . . . college . . . and get off welfare. So I applied and went to a business college. I got an associate degree as a medical-office assistant. It was during this period I had my second son and worked at a dermatology office. In fact it was the lady with sclerosis who got me the job. The owners were Christians. At that time I wasn't a Christian, and I was rebellious. They would ask me to come to the private prayer meetings they had before work began. And I told them, "I barely get there on time, so I don't think I'll be able to do that." It just seemed it was an issue after that, but I worked there for a year.

Then my boyfriend asked me what I was gonna do

since I didn't have a job. I said, "I don't know." But he said, "Once you went to college, why don't you go again?" And I think, Well, maybe I can. I also believe what it was—when I worked for that lady who said to me that I should go to college, she was trying to tell me that I could better myself. And she was right. I wish I could see her and tell her, she was right. But at the time that's not where my head was. I just thought she was being overbearing and stepping over into my personal business, which I didn't think she should. So I just let it go out one ear.

But I did enroll in the university. My first son was seven and my second was three when I started. I didn't even know what I was going to be. The lady I worked for would tell me, "You have a caring heart, so why don't you do nursing?" And then I would tell her, "No, I'm not gonna do nursing because that's all what women do. I want to do something different." But I ended up doing nursing, and I'm glad about it. I completed four years at the university and received the associate's degree in nursing at graduation. I went off welfare when I got my first job as a registered nurse in the hospital on the rehab floor for traumatic brain injuries and for automobile-accident and orthopedic patients. During that time it was pretty good. I hadn't got married, but me and my boyfriend still lived together. I stayed on at the hospital for ten years. Then I did home-health nursing for a year. I didn't like that. Then I did psychiatric nursing for six months, and I didn't like that. Then I got a job at BlueCross BlueShield. Now, I'm a case manager in a hospital.

When I finished my nursing degree, I had lived eleven years out of wedlock with my boyfriend. I had two children by him, went to a business college, worked, got a university degree—and he was on drugs the whole time. He was a crack addict. I wasn't on drugs—I didn't have a desire to be. I'd go to court with him, and the judge would say, "How is it that you are not involved?" I'd say, "I don't know how. I think it's because I see how it does people, and I just didn't have a desire to do it. I just don't know why, but I never had the desire to do that. So God, He just kept me." That's how I put it. I guess He know that if I did it, I probably wouldn't make it—not that I didn't smoke marijuana. I did smoke marijuana and did drink beer during that time; yet I still went to school, and I was still able to maintain keeping my kids. And probably I could have did much better if I didn't do stuff like that, but I did.

And it was a terrible time in my life. I went through a whole lot of things; but God kept me through all that happened—the Lord kept me. My husband was in and out of jail. He stole my money to where I couldn't pay my rent and stuff. But different people would help me out—my brothers and sister would help me out. If he took the money for the drugs or whatever, his family would help. Then it got to the point where they said, if I was gonna continue to stay with him, then they're not gonna help me. And I couldn't blame them, but I was upset about that. My mom would watch my kids anytime I need her to watch them—I will say that. She's a great mom. She has her faults, but she'd watch my kids while I went to college. I also had them in day care—the system paid for it a lot of times. And then when I got stable—got my RN and got saved the very next year—everything just changed. My boyfriend got off drugs and was a different person. God changed him. He was in jail, and he was facing a lot of time. A lot of people in jail say they've found God—because, of course, they want to get out—but he really did find God.

He told me he was reading his Bible, and that would make me sad because I started going to church and he couldn't be there. I was having a hard time dealing with that, even though we weren't married. When he said to me that he got baptized in the Holy Ghost there at the jail, I thought he was just talking. But he said that the Lord told him he was going to come home even though he was facing like, I think, five years. And his lawyer was telling him that he needed to take a plea, but he wouldn't because he said he wasn't guilty of what they were saying he was guilty of. To make a long story short, I went to court with him, and I looked up—they had studio lights—I thought I seen a lion and a angel. And I was like, What does that mean? And I heard the judge say to my boyfriend that he's been in jail so much that he was gonna be sent to prison. Then the judge said, "We'll recess for lunch." So I was just tore up. But then when we came back from recess, the judge said that he didn't know why, but he's gonna let my boyfriend out of jail. The DA got so upset about that, and they was arguing with the judge; but the judge still let him out. And so I looked at that as the lion meant there's gonna be war, and the angel covering it was Jesus. And I never forgot that because I kept seeing that, and I thought I was kinda losing my mind. I think, Is that real? But I felt like that was God's way of showing me (at that time) He was real, because I was just new in my faith.

When my boyfriend got out, he was a changed person. Basically, even though he had been in the home before, he wasn't a father figure to my children from '83 to '95 because he was on drugs. And I don't know how I stayed with him, but I did. I think it was because of my low self-esteem. He was never abusive to me. He would even tell me to leave because he didn't think he could kick the habit. But I just felt I seen he had a good heart, and I didn't have the strength to leave. I give God all the credit. But even after my boyfriend got out of jail, he stayed gone for over a week—I hadn't seen him in a week. And people had been inviting me to church, and I had been going; but he hadn't. Then that one particular Sunday morning, he came in as I was getting ready for church, and he said he was going to church too. Of course I was upset with him, but I just didn't say anything to him and didn't care if he went or not. But we ended up going to church, and we got saved on that same day—not planned, it just happened. And our lives have never been the same since. He's been the best father. That's why I know for sure those drugs are a demonic spirit that takes over people's lives—people that are not like that.

I have a brother that's dear to me. Him and my husband ran together. They are the same age, and they grew up together. They were on drugs together. That's why I have a passion for my brother, even though he has done some real terrible things and has kept getting in trouble. I still have passion that things for him can be turned around.

My other brothers and sister are pretty successful. My second brother is married and has two kids. He has a good job, and his wife has a good job. My younger brother has been in the military and now works at a local industry. He's got a wife and kids. My sister is married, her husband works, and they have kids. She never gave my mom any problems. The only one of my siblings that gave my mother problems, as I've said, was my brother that's near me. He's very intelligent, and he went to college as well. But the drugs overtook him.

So whatever environment a person's in, they have to make choices. And I was just fortunate enough not to have made a choice that caused me to have a life that would be detrimental and not productive. My husband says that jail took him off the street. It took him to a place he didn't like—he didn't like being told what to do, he didn't like the circumstances. He told me he prayed that they wouldn't let him out until he was ready. He didn't want to hurt us anymore, he didn't want to hurt his mom. A person has to have a good heart to do that. Hopefully, being in jail has helped my oldest brother too. Hopefully, he's tired of it. I don't know.

Well, after we got saved, my boyfriend backslid for about a couple of months, went back out in the street, and ended back in jail. I think he was in jail for six months or so. I bought him a Bible to read while he was in jail, and he would read it every day, he said. And they ended up calling him "Reverend Do-Right" because he stopped doing some of the things that they do in jail. And he was really trying to get his life together. He tells people all the time, "Sometime you need to go to a place where God can get your attention. You could be murdered or murder somebody, or whatever."

He believes that, he firmly believes that. He finally got out, and he hasn't been back since. He became a pastor. I think our faith is the main thing that helped us through all these times. And I think God just had a plan. I believe God has a plan for everybody's life, and this was His plan for me, even though other people couldn't see it. Everybody from my family to my friends—everybody—said, "Why do you put up with that?" I couldn't tell you the reason, just that it was love. There was times that I did think I was gonna leave, but I just didn't. I had to pray to God, "If he isn't for me, then You remove him because I can't do it." And what He did was put him in jail. So there we are.

My second brother also went to prison. He liked to make himself be bigger than he was and do things out of peer pressure. But he was the backbone of the family, like he was our father. He dropped out of high school and didn't finish, but he got a job. He would give my mom money, and he would give us money. He was very independent, like he would walk to his job that probably took him an hour or two, even in the cold and snow. He walked one time a hundred miles from another city, when his car broke down, rather than call anybody—that's the type of person he was. He became a manager in a store, but some people he knew sold him a sawed-off shotgun. The person that sold it got in trouble and must have told on my brother because investigators come to his house and found the gun. They said he wasn't supposed to have that kind of gun; and even though he had no record, he would have to do time. He'd never been in no trouble, everybody liked him, and we got good lawyers. But they said, it didn't matter because it was federal. And he had to go to a federal prison for a couple of years. He'll do anything for anybody; but from that experience, I think, he's changed. He doesn't want to be around family no more, hardly. I don't know what happened, but it just tore us up. I don't know. That's been a while back that it happened . . . I'd say ten years. He has a family now, but he doesn't call my mom. Me and him was the closest, but he doesn't call me no more. He still works, got a house, got a family; but I think it did something to him.

The third brother, he never got into trouble. He was a business man from the start. He was the first one of us who had a car, at the age of sixteen. He got a job and said he knew how to save money and budget. And that's what he did. He enlisted and went into the military for four years; and when he got out, he started with a big company and has been there now for almost thirty years.

So I believe, though my family grew up from humble beginnings, most of us are successful. We might not have everything that we want, but I feel like we're productive citizens—except the one brother. And he can still be productive as well if he can stay off the drugs. He's really a friendly, outgoing person. He gets along with anybody. He just got around the wrong friends. I believe too that he had an experience that changed things for him. When he was about thirteen, he was riding the school bus home, and a girl called him the N-word. He hit her and busted her nose. And that was the first encounter he had with the police. And they took him, and we didn't know what happened to him for days. And when he came back, he was different. He never said what happened to him. We asked him if they beat him up or whatever. And he would say, "I'm all right." So I don't know if that experience caused him to change. My mom tried to call, and they wouldn't give no information. And finally they let him out. And we were getting threatening phone calls from the person's family, that they were gonna kill us and this and that. They were white. He hit her because she called him the name, and he shouldn't have responded that way—he probably shouldn't, but he did. And he got charged, and he ended up in juvenile court for that. My mom had to take him to those juvenile hearings. And then after that it seemed like he just kept getting into trouble. Later in high school he got less in sports and more in with the wrong people. He started drinking and started getting on the drugs. Just downhill from there. He went to a small local college on a scholarship. He was a good athlete in baseball, football, and basketball. He was probably doing marijuana then, probably from peer pressure. I remember the first time somebody introduced me to alcohol. They was older than me, and they were like, "I'm gonna give you some of this . . . this is Kool-Aid . . . you'll like it . . . just take some." Then come to find out it was liquor. If somebody introduces you to it, then you either get addicted or you don't. But I'm sure somebody introduced him to something, and it just went from there.

Even though my brother seemed changed after the bus incident, he didn't carry any hate toward anybody. He still always tries to help people. Even for some of the guys he was in jail with, he would ask me to bring clothes or something. He's got that kind of personality. He's always had white friends as well as black. He doesn't feel any negativity towards anybody. He's just like that. But he doesn't realize either that there are some problems. He always had white ladies, and he had some black ladies too. But when he's out on drugs, he's mostly white ladies. And most of them was on drugs. He's going with a white girl now, but I don't think she's on any drugs. In our household, we didn't look at people differently—I mean, people was people. He's never had any problem in getting along. He don't meet no strangers. Now, if I needed protection, that would be different. I remember one time going to the club, and he was there. This guy was trying to mess with me, and my brother just came up, and he said, "Are you messing with my sister?"—at the same time punching his palm with his fist. He is just that kind of guy. He will take up for his family. Just like with my mom when me and him was talking about her, he would say, "You know how Mom is. She's old, just let it go. You'll feel bad if she dies." He's just that kind of person, to pull you together. He's got a good heart, he's got the biggest heart.

For me personally, I've never had any problems with racial prejudice. I always felt like, you treat me nice, I treat you nice. Every school I went to was integrated—first grade, elementary, all the way up. I really didn't have any issues. Now, when we were in the Project, it was all segregated. It was all black in that project. Another project in a different area of town was all white. Now they're both integrated. Of course, I could tell there were people who were prejudiced, but I've never really let it bother me. I didn't feel any discrimination because of my clothes or anything. Sometimes the clothes might wear out, and I'd have to wait to get more clothes. Then of course I'd feel a little bit bad, but I never really had an issue. I never had to fight or say something to somebody. I know there was fights and stuff; but, as far as me, I wasn't involved in that. I was just to myself. I was the type of person that's kinda shy, and I stayed to myself mainly. I had a couple of friends and hung out with them, but other than that I was real, real shy. I really didn't say anything to anybody. It wasn't until, probably, I got saved that I start voicing my opinions. Anybody could walk over me. That was just the way it was. I've never had problems with anybody. I tried to stay out of anybody's business or to stay out of the way. That's me. And I never did feel, either, a lot of prejudice from others. I might just been ignorant to the fact, but I didn't really feel that way. I didn't hardly have no white friends going to school—my friends was the ones that live in the Project. That's just the way it was. We hung with who we knew. The only time I start associating with a white friend is when I moved out of my mom's house. There was a white girl that I started hanging out with that I would call a good friend. My mama didn't raise us up prejudiced. She might say, "You better be careful if the police stop you—be respectful." But she didn't raise us up prejudiced, and that's why I think we don't have a problem. You treat others just like you want to be treated—that's the way we was taught.

Even though I have been where I personally never had to deal with racism, now it seems like it's kinda come back. Even in the hospitals, I've heard remarks such as, "Do they still allow these 'niggers' to come in here?" I've needed to go into a room and take care of someone where they'll say, "I don't want you to take care of me." I can just feel the animosity. On the other hand, I have peers and coworkers that we can talk together without any prejudice. It seems like some things are stirring up that's getting ideas in people's minds. Or it may be that it's just been covered up, and it's trying to come out again. I don't know. I would say, as a black woman, I know there's prejudiced people; but I'll still treat them with dignity. "If you don't want me to take care of you," I tell them, "let me get somebody else that you feel more comfortable with." There is racism, there is some division. I work in a hospital where a lot of people come from back-hills Virginia—Grundy, Pennington Gap, Weber City—and a lot of them make it known they don't really care for black people. Then there's some that do. So you can't judge everybody by the color. I just judge them how they act towards me.

You do see racism on the media more, and it's infiltrating people's minds—that's part of it. And it does seem like racism is on a rise. I feel a noticeable change, but I wasn't feeling the change till maybe the last couple of years. I'm sure there was stuff underground. But now some people feel like black people are saying how they've been discriminated against; so, I guess, they want to come out and say how they've been discriminated against. Now it's just a mess because nobody's trying really to fix the issue. You have people in the government, I feel, that's not helping; so it's gonna be a mess. I just pray that we don't go back and that somehow we can get it worked out. My son is married to a white girl, and there are some times they get treated differently when they go into restaurants. And they have a child, so I'm kinda concerned about that.

But I think our family's just normal people that have the same type of problems that everybody has. We just have to learn to cope with them. We may cope with them in a different way, but we're still coping, still got problems, still got issues. We just want to try to do what's right. I like my life. I don't like everything that happens in it, but I can't say I'm bitter.

And I repeat, as I'll tell anybody, I loved the Project. You don't hear that, but when I get up in church, I say, "I came from the Project, and that was the best experience I ever had." Before that I could see the rats and the things in the house that would just terrify me; and I hated that house, I just hated it. When I came to the Project, there was a cleaner place of living. I had my friends, I just liked it. I didn't really have any bad experience. Actually, it helped me, it gave me insight in what I do now. I meet people that come from the same type of environment that I do, and I meet people who think they're better than them—and I will be the one that says, "You know, I came from the projects." And it kind of puts a damper to it. I think that's why I was there, because I'm able to see both sides. Even though they may be low down, they were a child at one time; and they chose the wrong choices. My part is to try encourage them and say, "Even though you're making wrong choices, that don't mean you have to stay there."

So that's where I'm also at with my brother and his drugs. Even my mama wouldn't encourage me to help him. I was the only one, because . . . I don't know why . . . I guess because my husband was an addict. I know that is not the people they really are. It's an evil spirit that comes and possesses them to do what they do. That's how I have to look at it. Now, I will say that sometimes it is them. There are things you can do or not do, and you have the ability to make a choice. I had to get to that point with my husband, and he said I was right. But then with my brother, I had to slip and not tell my husband that I was trying to help him. My husband would get mad at me since he felt my brother could do better, the same as he had done. But everybody's not the same. So I struggled with that. And I think my brother one time said to me, "You've changed"—because I had to set boundaries. I said to him, "Listen, I can't do it anymore, unless you make some changes. Every time you call me, you're needing something. And it's not helping you if I'm just being a codependent to you." So I have to learn how, even though I love him, to set boundaries—just like I'm setting boundaries with my mom. And now, he doesn't call me like he normally do, and he's not asking me for anything lately. He only does that when he starts getting on these drugs. But now he's like, I'm trying to get a house. I'm going to church. I'm this and that. So I know he has a good heart. That's just what I believe—I've seen it in my husband. I feel like I have discernment of people, and I think that's a gift God gave me. And the thing I do want to get across is, it's not where you live, it's where *you're* at. That means, wherever you live, it is not what the environment is, you make a choice of how you want to live.

Now, projects like Chicago, I might have a different perspective—or if something had happened to me in the Project. But nothing happened to me, so that's why I feel like I do. And when I go to different cities, I want to go to the projects, because I have a connection with them. My brother is like, "Sure they aren't gonna rob you there?" Well, I know that my going there could be poor judgment— things are happening. But just to tell you my honest-to-God's truth, my life too was not like I wanted it at all times— whose is? But I've made the best out of what I had.

Right now I'm in a dilemma as far as my spiritual walk—seeing where I'm gonna be. My husband got hurt on his job and went on disability now for probably about ten years. When he became disabled, he started working in the church; but then he got sick and was out at least two and a-half months. It was a very small congregation, and no one came to check on things. The owner didn't fix anything; and the building got in a bad state, the bills got behind—so we had to let the building go. Now my husband's retired, and he's having a hard time dealing with it. I feel like he's going through a little depression, and I have been kind of despondent myself, kinda discouraged. I wonder did *we* fail, or is it something *God* wants us to do differently? I don't know. But I know God's gonna take care of me if I keep my faith. As long as I try to read my Word and continue going to church, I feel I'll stay on the right path. But I don't know exactly, as far as what God has planned for me. I used to be a Sunday school teacher and used to do speaking engagements. I done pretty much everything in the church—cleaned the church, do whatever needed to be done. And I kinda miss that now. First, I said I wasn't gonna miss it, because of the people—the people were getting on my nerves, just like Moses.

Other than that, of course I'd like to have more finances to make the bills. But I have three grandchildren. My youngest son lives in another city. Him and his wife is a teacher. And my other son, he lives near me. He's married as well. He now works at a factory job, but he's been hurt on two jobs and had two surgeries. He's getting older, so I tell him to go to school to use his mind instead of his body. And he's trying to do that.

I'm fifty-seven, and I'm thinking about early retirement, if I can make the bills meet. Then I'm just gonna lavish on my grandbabies. I don't know what the next chapter is, but I guess whatever I'm looking forward to is to happen. Whichever way I go, I'll try, I'll try.

Concluding Remarks

As the reader may observe, the three women in the portraits presented are both similar and diverse in various ways. They come from and live in the same area on the western edge of the Blue Ridge Mountains, which is designated by the Appalachian Region Commission as South Central Appalachia. The portraits are not sociological case studies of the speakers or of the areas from which they come; rather they are personal stories of three women that reveal their personalities, social backgrounds, and the evolution of their present states of being. They are interesting stories of individuals who (not emanating from any single group and not unique to the area) represent a certain stratum of Appalachian women whose lives are to a great extent outside the norm. The three women have taken divergent roads, sometimes of their own choices and sometimes roads effected by race, gender, economics, beliefs, traditions, limited options, genetics, or other influences thrust upon them. And the road taken by each, as stated in the familiar quotation, "has made all the difference" in their lives. Other individuals or strata might well have been chosen or included, but the voices of these women have much to say that enlightens us and that serves well the designed scope of this work.

Like dramatic soliloquies, these self-portraits address their audience directly. The women do not tell what the responses should be to them personally or to their lives. They do not say what their stories mean. When they stop speaking, readers are left with their own intellectual and emotional responses to what they have heard. Following some theatrical performances, a selected individual provides critical analyses of the play. The analyses can be insightful and helpful. On the other hand, they can overstate critical perceptions and restrict the personal intellectual and emotional responses of the audience. A case in point is the statement by none other than the remarkable Old Vic player himself, Sir Laurence Olivier, at the beginning of his film *Hamlet*—it has focal design, no doubt, but it is nonetheless a restrictive commentary on one of the world's most complex plays: "This is the tragedy of a man who could not make up his mind."

There are many studies toward the understanding of Appalachia. Regrettably some of the studies purport to be comprehensive, although based on a limited area of Appalachia and on little attention to its diverse people. Critical analyses are important, and of course no single approach to the understanding of Appalachia is sufficient unto itself.

Yet essential to the understanding of Appalachia is listening to what Appalachians themselves have to say. What is asked of readers in the portraits of these three women is to listen carefully and sensitively to their voices. Much is revealed of the heart of Appalachia by listening to them, as well as to individuals of other diverse areas and strata of the region—they are all part of the whole.